AF568123

INDUSTRIAL MANAGEMENT
(WITH CASE STUDIES)

INDUSTRIAL MANAGEMENT
(WITH CASE STUDIES)

By

Dr. Rabi Narayan Misra

&

Dr. Rookesh Kumar Misra

DISCOVERY PUBLISHING HOUSE PVT. LTD.

INDIA

Published by:

Namit Wasan

DISCOVERY PUBLISHING HOUSE PVT. LTD.

4383/4B, Ansari Road, Darya Ganj
New Delhi-110 002 (India)
Phone : +91-11-23279245, 43596064-65
Fax : +91-11-23253475
E-mail : discoverypublishinghouse@gmail.com
namitwasan9@gmail.com
sales@discoverypublishinggroup.com
web : www.discoverypublishinggroup.com

***First Edition:* 2017**

ISBN: 978-93-5056-857-6

Industrial Management (With Case Studies)

Printed at:
Infinity Imaging Systems
Delhi

Preface

Industrial Management is a good system of management which discuss about human capital, its need in the various activities from time to time. Payment for human services and performance of each individual to be measured by taking different tools. The system, of "Work Audit" is to be adopted for proper and effective payment from top to bottom.

Payment should be given to a individual, according to his work performance in an organization, if the performance is not upto the mark, 'feedback' should be provided to increase the work standard.

This book is very much helpful to HRM department of organizations, MBA students, Commerce students of different universities, Non-government organizations, labour officers and to the research scholars who are dealing with 360 degree of Performance Appraisal.

—Dr. R.N. Misra
—Dr. Rookesh K. Misra

Contents

SECTION-A

CHAPTER

1 Nature and Concept of Human Resource Management

Introduction

The advent of the era of liberalization and globalization along with the advancements in information technology (IT) has transformed the world around us. It has brought to centre stage the importance of human resources, more than ever before. The purpose of human resource management (HRM) is to enable appropriate deployment of human resources.

In a competitive scenario, effective utilization of human resources has become necessary and the primary task of organizations is to identify, recruit, and channel competent human resources into their business operations for improving productivity and functional efficiency. Several authors have tried to understand the meaning of human resources and one of the comprehensive definitions was given by Leon C. Megginson, who described human resources as the sum total of the knowledge, abilities and attitudes of all the employees of an organization. Effective utilization of human resources would lead to both accomplishment of individual and organizational goals and creation of assets at the national level. It is in this context that development of human resources, which involves continuous honing of employee skills, has become vital for the survival of organizations, let alone growth and development.

Definitions

Management has been defined as control and creation of a technological and human environment that can support optimal utilization of resources and competencies for achieving organizational goals. Management has also been variously defined as development of people; the process of decision-making and control over actions of human beings; planning, organizing, and controlling of people and resources; the process of accomplishing the desired organizational objectives; effective utilization of available resources for delivery of services and goods, etc.

It is in this backdrop that we will try to understand the broad definitions of human resource management given by various experts.

Process consisting of four functions—acquisition, development, motivation and maintenance of human resources.

[David A. Decenzo and Stephen P. Robbins]

Personnel management is the planning, organizing, directing and controlling of the procurement, development, compensation, integration., maintenance and separation of human resources to the end that individual, organizational and societal objectives are accomplished. [Edward Filippo]

Recent literature on knowledge management and creation of people-centric partnership suggests that there is a need to increasingly integrate information technology (IT) with human competence for optimum utilization of both kinds of resources. An analysis of various definitions indicates that human resource management includes the following activities:

- aligning the HR strategy with the corporate strategy of the organization
- working for the well-being of all the employees
- developing employee competencies
- sourcing, deployment, and development of human resources for optimal utilization
- employee empowerment
- performance management .

Human resource management can be defined as a strategic and coherent approach to the management of the most valued assets of an organization, i.e., people, who individually and collectively contribute to the organizational objectives. Storey (1989) has made a distinction between 'hard' and 'soft" versions of HRM. The hard approach focuses on the quantitative and strategic aspects of managing the human resources. It is a rational approach, which deals with human resources like any other economic factor. It emphasizes the need for managing people to enhance their contribution to improving the quantitative advantage of the organization. It aims at protecting the, interests of the management and building a strong corporate culture by internalization of the mission and value statements of the organization.

The soft approach to HRM, whose roots can be traced to the human resource school, emphasizes factors such as communication, motivation and leadership. It treats employees as the essential means of realizing organizational objectives rather than mere objects. It focuses on engendering commitment among employees by winning their hearts. The functions of HRM include:

- facilitating the retention of skilled and competent employees,
- building the competencies of human resources by facilitating continuous learning and development,
- developing and implementing high performance work systems,
- developing management practices that engender high commitment,
- developing practices which foster team work and flexibility,
- making the employees feel that they are valued and rewarded for their contribution, and
- facilitating management of workforce diversity and availability of equal opportunities to all.

Human Resource Management—History

The evolution of HRM can be traced back to the HR movement in the ancient period. However, in the modern age, i.e., up to

1930s, it was referred to as personnel management and the focus was on the employer-employee relations. Studies on HR were initially guided by Taylor's scientific management principles and then graduated through the Hawthorne studies to the behavioural school based on the theories of Abraham Maslow, Herzberg, and Douglas McGregor.

Various developments in the 21st century heralded the arrival of the knowledge and IT era. During the initial phases, IT was perceived as an all-pervasive phenomenon and attempts were made to tune all organizational processes to this development. However, the experience of a large number of organizations both at me global and the national level has led to the realization that IT has to play only a supportive role in achieving organizational objectives and for this purpose an organization has to focus on its three core areas, i.e., people, processes, and performance (called the 3 Ps).

HRM and the 3 Ps

People: It is now an established fact that the core strength of an organization lies in its human resources and it would not be an exaggeration to say that all other resources can be replaced except the human resources.

Processes: Organizational processes evolve over a period of time and often these are treated as sanctimonious. The justification for doing so is the belief that what has worked so well in the past would work in the future as well. However, in the fast changing world, much emphasis is laid on flexibility and adaptability. Also, in the past, it would have been a Herculean task to re-engineer the processes, but in an IT-enabled environment, re-engineering of processes at the server level would simultaneously and effortlessly lead to re-engineering across the organization.

Performance: The existence of an organization is primarily dependent on its ability to create value and continuously increase the rate of return on investment (ROI). The two pillars supporting the performance of an organization are people and IT. The integration of these two factors plays the pivotal role in improving the performance of an organization at both individual and organizational levels. IT helps in documenting the knowledge pool in an organization and making it available to the employees through intranet, etc. Further, management of knowledge workers is different from that of conventional employees as the level of intelligence and maturity of knowledge workers is higher and hence, they expect greater levels of flexibility and freedom in their work area.

HRM and Its Evolution in India

The history of HRM in India dates back to the early 1980s when Mr Udai Pareek and Mr. T.V. Rao championed the cause of the HRM movement. The early adopters of the HRM movement include public sector enterprises such as Bharat Heavy Electricals Limited (BHEL), State Bank of India, etc. Initially, Indian organizations used to have an industrial relations (IR) department, which was subsequently re-christened as the personnel & IR department, with the welfare department as one of its sub-departments. The personnel department predominantly suited the blue-collar employees since their general awareness and educational levels were low and the approach was more of administrative nature. The growing importance of the service sector in the Indian economy has also highlighted the importance of change in approach by the personnel and administrative departments. The profile of an employee in the new scenario has the following features:

- Employees are mostly in their mid-twenties or early thirties.
- All employees are educated and their level of general awareness is high.
- Employees are more committed to the profession than to the organization.
- The rates of attrition and the level of mobility of employees among the organizations are high.

The organizations have to compete for scarce resources, the most important among them being the human resources, more so in the case of the service sector. This has called for the radical transformation of personnel and administrative departments into human resource departments to reflect the human facet of organizations. A glance at the structure of various Indian organizations indicates that the majority of the organizations have rechristened their personnel and administrative departments as human resource development (HRD) departments. However, this transformation into the HRM mode is at various stages in different organizations. The progressive players and market leaders, especially in the IT and service sectors, have fully adopted this approach while other players are in the process of adoption. The transformed HR department performs the following functions:

- participating in the strategizing sessions of business policy
- preparing the HR strategies in coordination with the corporate strategies
- implementing the various HR policies and practices including HR planning, recruitment and induction, compensation structuring, career planning, competence mappingj performance management, etc.

The flow of activities in the HRM function is diagrammatically represented in Figure 1.1.

Overall, the HR department has outgrown its mere functional role and has come to assume the responsibility of building the brand for the company to attract the best available talent in the market and also to retain the existing talent. This helps in reducing the recruitment cost and the replacement cost apart from reducing the attrition rates, which helps the organization to complete its projects in time.

HRM and IT

The advent of information technology has changed the competitive landscape of the corporate world. IT influences the corporate world through three factors:

- *Information technology practices:* It denotes the capabilities of a company to effectively utilize IT applications and infrastructure to support its business processes and operations.

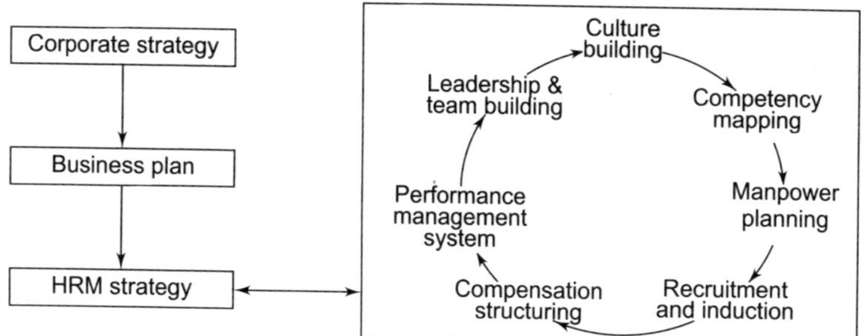

Fig. 1.1 Flow of Activities in the HRM Function

- *Information management practices:* It denotes the organizational capabilities to manage the entire information life cycle, i.e., sensing, collecting, organizing, processing, and maintaining information.
- *Information behaviours/values (IBV):* It indicates the organizational capabilities to promote behaviours and values that facilitate the effective use of information.

The first one, i.e., IT practices, is more in the domain of IT specialists, while the HR department has to deal with the second and the third, respectively. HR managers have to work in close coordination with the IT head for creating awareness about the information management practices. The key challenge is to define and communicate the information behaviours/ values expected from the employees. More importantly, HR managers have to initiate an organizational-culture building exercise for internalization and adoption of the desired values.

HRM and Competency Building

Two of the recent and widely used terms among HRM professionals are 'competency building' and 'competency mapping' among the employees. Beginners in the subject would wonder what could be the importance of the so-called 'competence' in organizational context and more so from the

HRM perspective. Michael Porter, who shared his path-breaking research findings through his book *Competitive Advantage*, has proposed that the competitive advantage for an organization is dependent on its distinctive capabilities to use the available resources for value creation. One of the fundamental and generic models of competitive advantage is shown in Figure 1.2.

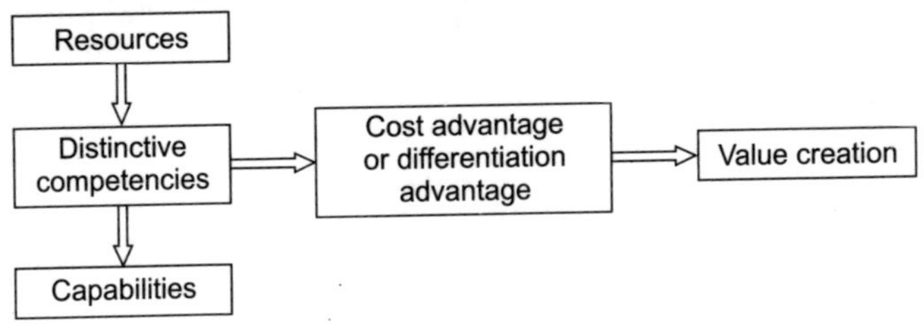

Fig. 1.2 Model of Competitive Advantage

The model shown in Fig. 1.2 indicates that the activities of an organization are based on various resources, such as material, human, financial, etc., and the capabilities would vary from one company to another. For instance, L&T Ltd has the capabilities to undertake and execute large-scale construction projects in a time-bound manner. Its distinctive capabilities are those that are unique to the company. In the same way, Reliance has the capabilities to undertake and complete large-scale petrochemicals projects as a strategy towards forward and backward integration and gaining economies-of-scale advantage over its rivals. Depending on its distinctive capabilities, an organization can have cost advantage or differentiation advantage. Indian IT companies are typical examples, which started with cost advantage and are gradually moving towards differentiation advantage to meet the competition in American and European markets. At the end of the entire process, an organization should be able to creat 'value' for ail its stakeholders, i.e., employees, shareholders, investors, etc.

HRM and Performance Management

In the present competitive scenario, one of the foremost challenges for the organizations and more specifically for the HR department, is to facilitate performance of individuals to realize the organizational objectives. Planning for the performance is the first step towards performance management.

Performance planning can be defined as systematic outlining of tasks/activities to be carried out by the employees during the specific period so that they are able to contribute towards accomplishment of organizational goals. The planning process involves aspects such as the time frame, activities/area-wise targets, tasks to be coordinated, etc. In short, performance planning emphasizes individual contribution *vis-a-vis* the organizational goals. The scope of performance planning in an organization covers its entire set of employees. Further, there has been an eternal debate as to whether performance planning should be top-down, bottom-up, or both ways. The process of performance planning involves various activities such as task analysis and/or activity analysis, analysis of key performance areas (KPAs), analysis of key result areas (KRAs), tasks and target identification, preparation of activity plans/action plans, goal setting exercises, etc.

Practitioners and researchers after prolonged debate have come to the conclusion that there is no generic and universally applicable performance management model and the approach would depend on the specificities of individual organizations. The various aspects of devising the performance management system (PMS) of an organization are:

- *Results and output:* The foremost aspect is measurability of the output; for instance, the results achieved have to be defined clearly in terms of number, figures, etc. It is important for the appraiser as well as the appraisee to state clearly the yardsticks for measurement.
- *Input dimensions:* They indicate the activities/tasks to be carried out by individual employees for achieving the tasks set or defined. The other aspects to be considered are time frame and input quality. As it is said, a task well planned is half the success achieved and the ability of an employee lies in accurately assessing and arranging the requirements for successful completion.

- *Time dimension:* Apart from the objectives/goals/targets, in a competitive environment, it is critical for employees to complete the jobs assigned to them in time. Often, people tend to evaluate performance without taking into account the time aspect, but for a comprehensive and objective analysis, performance has to be assessed against time. Further, while evaluating performance, it is essential to analyse the time taken by the same employee or another employee to complete a similar job under similar circumstances.
- *Focus dimension:* Performance also has a focus dimension and it would depend upon the area of focus, which varies from job to job. For instance, in case of a trainer, the areas of focus would be self-learning as well as facilitating the learning of the trainees. In case of marketing managers, the focus area would be gaining market share in the existing as well as new markets, etc.
- *Input-output relationship:* It indicates die effort *vis-a-vis* performance. In this sense, die measure for performance would be whether an employee could deliver higher levels of performance for the same input, which would imply improved levels of efficiency.
- *Role clarity and performance facilitation:* Often, employees are found lacking in performance due to lack of clarity about their roles and responsibilities. In other words, they lack clear understanding of their job profile and die responsibilities. The immediate superior is also responsible for such a situation since it is his or her responsibility to see that the employees concerned have a clear idea of their job profile and responsibilities.

HRM and Leadership Building

Many successful organizations are of the view that the success, to a large extent, is dependent on having the right leaders at the right time. The debate here is whether leadership should emerge on its own in an organization or the organization should make a conscious attempt to build leaders for its future growth. *Prima facie*, both the approaches are equally valid for building successful leadership. For instance, when we look at some of the successful enterprises, such as Reliance, Infosys, etc., it is observed that the growth and development of the these organizations is mainly because of the foresight and leadership capabilities of their founders, i.e., Dhirubhai Ambani and Narayana Murthy, respectively.

Similarly, when we analyse the emergence of great historical leaders, we find that they did not establish their leadership overnight but through a sustained and long-term process. For instance, in our country, we have had leaders like Mahatma Gandhi, who from his humble background rose to become one of the all-time great leaders of the world. On the contrary, Mrs Indira Gandhi, who belonged to one of the politically most influential families of the country, also became a great leader over a period of time.

Some of the key issues in the emergence of leaders are discussed below:

Knowledge: Socrates thought that professional or technical competence is a prerequisite for holding the position of leadership. It is a general tendency of people to follow somebody who knows what to do in a crisis. The three important qualities that attract people towards leaders are authority of position/ rank, authority of personality, and authority of knowledge. Socrates clearly emphasized the latter. Kautilya, one of the renowned ancient Indian strategists, has given art extensive description of successful leaders and their essential traits.

Experience: Leaders are born rarely and often are products of their times. It would not be an exaggeration to say that the times of trials and tribulations in history have provided excellent opportunities for the emergence of leaders. Nelson Mandela had to struggle for about three decades to emancipate himself and also fellow compatriots in South Africa.

Action-orientedness: Mere intellectual thought and foresight would not make a good leader since the followers constantly look forward to their leader for command and orientation. As the saying goes, a leader should lead by example first and then, after developing die followers, adopt the approach of leading from behind.

People management capability: One of the essential qualities of successful leaders is to convince and carry along their subordinates on an identified course of action to realize the collective objectives. The prolonged freedom struggle did not deter the people of India from continuing to believe in the leadership of Mahatma Gandhi. Similar is a case of Nelson Mandela. In Myanmar, Aung San Sui Kyi, the leader who has been fighting for democratic rights of people in her country for more than a decade, has many loyal followers in spite of the oppression of the military junta.

Foresight and acumen: Leaders should be able to predict the future with conviction so that the followers remain patient and persistent till the end. Moses in ancient Christian mythology was one such leader, who led his followers on the path of truth in spite of many a struggle.

Leaders should learn from the above historical examples while establishing leadership-building practices in an organization. A proactive HR strategy, which attempts to build good leaders, would have the following features:

- Recruitment policies that attract and retain the best talent in the country
- Job postings that provide challenging and learning assignments to prospective organizational leaders
- Career planning that facilitates growth of youngsters into organizational leadership positions
- Organizational-culture-building exercise that can promote parameters such as openness, transparency, honesty, and integrity of employees.

According to Socrates, a successful leader should have the following six skills:

- selecting the right man for the right job
- punishing the bad and rewarding the good
- winning the goodwill of subordinates

- attracting alliance and helpers
- keeping what they have gained
- working diligently and efficiently to fulfil their own responsibilities.

HR managers, while grooming prospective leaders, should attempt to inculcate the above skills in them. Lao Tzu, in his writings on leadership, has envisaged a humble leader who is neither self-assertive nor talkative. Alexander the great, die Greek emperor known for his charismatic leadership, used to march along with his soldiers on foot even in deserts and adverse conditions to maintain the unity and team spirit of his soldiers. This quality holds equally good in the organizational context, as the actions of leaders should speak for themselves.

HRM and Change Management

Change is inevitable in life and yet we feel comfortable and secure in an environment that is steady and unchanging and where the future does not appear uncertain. In case of organizations, the general tendency is to be complacent with policies and practices that have been successful in the past. Often organizations and individuals at the helm of affairs get into the delusion that past success is a guarantee of future success and one has to continue to adhere to policies and practices that have been successful in the past. It is for this reason that the list, of Fortune 500 companies of the world keeps changing every decade.

A cursory glance at the history of many of the successful organizations indicates that organizations that have been adaptive and change-oriented continue to be successful while those otherwise become a part of history. Adaptability and change orientation cannot be inculcated overnight, but organizations have to build practices to facilitate and nurture change management processes. In die contemporary scenario, organizations are faced with multi-faceted challenges, such *as* changes in technology, competition, etc., and increasingly face new challenges on account of change. It is important to note that though change has been prevalent in all times, of late die pace of change has become very rapid.

Some of the new challenges for the organizations are:

- customers and global operations demand 24 × 7 service
- technology facilitates any-location work possibilities
- geographical borders have been blurred and a virtual world has been created.

The above developments make the challenges of HR even more difficult. Human resource, which has been a staff function, has now assumed a strategic function, as it has to coordinate with other functional areas in forecasting the future and gearing up the human resources to meet the future challenges. Simultaneously, HR has the onerous task of convincing the top management to initiate and sustain change management programmes, which usually have initial debacles. Some of the challenges for HR personnel as regards change management are:

- facilitating the work-life balance for employees
- facilitating the culture change for employees
- competence mapping and building
- preparing career plans
- managing attritions
- managing cultural diversity
- sustaining and improving the productivity and creativity
- re-orienting the organizational practices and policies to suit die new generation employees.

In the context of work-life balance, die employees have to balance between work, home and community and HR personnel have the responsibility of facilitating it through:

- pragmatic awareness programmes
- facilitating their thinking both about work and non-work life streams
- education of managers to counsel and coach employees
- professional counselling directly by HR personnel for employees who are struggling to adjust

One of the important challenges in change management *vis-a-vis* HR functions is adapting organizations and employees to jobs and careers that have short life cycles. For this purpose, organizations as well as employees will have to frequently reinvent themselves through continuous learning and skill upgradation. The learning processes have to be synchronized in the sense that organizations and employees have to work in sync towards the same direction. In the present context, employees have a greater responsibility to continuously learn and upgrade themselves if they want to remain useful to the organization and progress in their careers.

All said and done, there is no universal approach to change management as the success of change initiatives is dependent on various factors, such as organizational culture, determination of the top management, proactiveness of the HR personnel.

Value-based Human Resource Strategy

Organizations in the competitive scenario are continuously faced with the necessity to create and sustain practices that facilitate value creation. The existence of organizations is largely dependent on creating outputs that mathematically outweigh the value of inputs, which in turn gives it the competitive advantage over its rivals. The HR has a key role in the entire process, which includes the following responsibilities:

- developing competitive advantage of organizations by proactively developing the business strategy
- contributing to creation and catering of shareholder value and, for this purpose, creating short-, medium-, and long-term strategies to facilitate cash generation
- developing the HR strategy as an integral part of the business strategy
- taking the top management or the CEO of the organization into confidence while formulating the HR strategy
- reorienting the processes, priorities, and skills of the HR department to facilitate and support the HR strategy as to value creation.

The essential components of an HR strategy are plans and programmes related to HR projects, intentions that crystallize into specific plans/projects, formal and informal arrangements in organizations to facilitate work processes.

CHAPTER

2 Performance Management

Early Days

The first recorded use of the term 'performance management' is in Beer and Ruh (1976). Their thesis was that 'performance is best developed through practical challenges and experiences on the job with guidance and feedback from superiors'. They described the performance-management system at Corning Glass Works, the aim of which was to help managers give feedback in a helpful and constructive way, and to aid in the creation of a development plan. The features of this system, which the authors said distinguished it from other appraisal schemes, were as follows:

- Emphasis on both development and evaluation.
- Use of a profile defining the individual's strengths and development needs.
- Integration of the results achieved with the means by which they have been achieved.
- Separation of development review from salary review.

Although this was not necessarily a model performance-management process, it did contain a number of characteristics still regarded as good practice.

The concept of Performance Management then lay fallow for some years, but began to emerge in the USA in the mid-1980s as a new approach to managing performance. However, one of the first books exclusively devoted to performance management was not published until 1987. He described what had become the accepted approach to performance management as follows:

Performance management is communication: a manager and an employee arrive together at an understanding of what work is to be accomplished, how it will be accomplished, how work is progressing towards desired results and finally, after effort is expended to accomplish the work, whether the performance has achieved the agreed-upon plan. The process recycles when the manager and employee begin planning what work is to be accomplished for the next performance period. Performance management is an umbrella term that includes performance planning, performance review and performance appraisal. Major work plans and appraisals are generally made annually. Performance review occurs whenever a manager and an employee confirm, adjust, or correct their understanding of work performance during routine work contacts.

In U.K. the first published reference to performance management was made at a meeting of the Institute of Personnel Management (IPM) Compensation Forum in 1987 by Don Beattie, then Personnel Director, ICL, who described how it was used as 'an essential contribution to a massive and urgent change programme in the organisation' and had become a part of the fabric of the business.

By 1990 performance management had entered the vocabulary of HRM in the UK as well as in the USA. Fowler (1990) defines what has become the accepted concept of performance management.

Management has always been about getting things done and good managers are concerned to get the right things done well. That in essence, is performance management—the organization of work to achieve the best possible results. From this simple viewpoint, performance management is not a system or technique. It is the totality of the day-to-day activities of all managers.

Performance Management Established

Full recognition of the existence of performance management was provided by the research project conducted the (then)

Institute of Personnel Management (1992). The following definition of performance management was produced as a result:

> A Strategy which relates to every activity of the organization set in the context of its human resources policies, culture, style and communication systems. The nature of the strategy depends on the organizational context and can vary from organization to organization.

It was suggested that what described was as a 'Performance Management System' (PMS) complied with the textbook definition when the following characteristics were met by the organization:

(*i*) It communicates a vision of its objectives to all its employees.

(*ii*) It sets departmental and individual performance targets that are related to wider objectives.

(*iii*) It conducts a formal review of progress towards these targets.

(*iv*) It uses the review process to identigy training, development and reward outcomes.

(*v*) It evaluates the whole process in order to improve effectiveness.

In addition, 'Performance Management Organisation':

(*a*) Express performance targets in terms of measurable outputs, accountabilities and training/learning targets.

(*b*) Use formal appraisal procedures as ways of communication performance requirements that are set on a regular basis.

(*c*) Link performance requirements to pay, especially for senior managers.

In the organization's with performance management systems, 85 per cent had performance pay and 76 per cent rated performance. The emphasis was on objective setting and reviews, which as the authors of the report noted, 'leaves something of a void when it comes to identifying development needs on a longer term bases. There is a danger with results orientated schemes and focusing excessively on what is to be achieved and ignoring.' It was noted that some organizations were moving in the direction of competency analysis, but not very systematically.

Two of the IPM researchers commented on the emergence of performance management systems as integrating processes that mesh various HRM activities with the business objectives of the organization. They identified two broad thrusts towards integration.

Reward driven integration, which emphasizes the role of performance pay in changing organizational behavior and tends to undervalue the part played by other human resource development (HRD) activities. This appeared to be the dominant mode of integration.

Development driven integration, which stresses the importance of HRD. Although performance pay may operate in these organizations' it is perceived to be complementary to HRD activities rather than dominating them.

Some of the interesting conclusions emerging from this research were that:

- 'No evidence was found that improved performance in the private sector is associated with the presence of formal performance management programmes.
- 'An overwhelming body of psychological research exists which makes clear that, as a way of enhancing individual performance, the setting of performance targets is inevitably a successful strategy.'
- 'The process of forming judgements and evaluations of individual performance is an almost continuous one. Most often it is a subconscious process, relying on subjective judgements based on incomplete evidence and spiced with an element of bias.'
- 'There was little consistency of view point on the motivating power of money. The majority of organisations

felt that the real motivators at management level were professional and personal pride in the standards achieved or loyalty to the organization and its aims, or peer pressure. One line manager commented that he was self-motivated. The money comes as a result of that, not as the cause of it. While the principle of pay for performance was generally accepted, the reservations were about putting it into proactive. It was often viewed as a good idea - especially for other people - but not something that, when implemented, seemed to breed either satisfaction or motivation.

- The focus has been on the splendid sounding notion of the performance orientated culture and of improving the bottom line and / or the delivery of services. Whilst this is well and good, the achievement of such ends has to be in concert with the aims and the development needs of individuals.

Why Performance Management?

Performance management arrived in the late 1980s partly as a reaction to the negative aspects of merit rating and management by objectives referred to earlier. Of course, it at first incorporated many of the elements of earlier approaches, for example, rating, objective setting and review, performance pay and a tendency towards trait assessment. Some of these features have changed and the new realities of performance management will be spelt out conceptually, however performance management is significantly different from previous approaches although in practice the term has often simply replaced 'Performance Appraisal', just as human resource management without any discernible change in approach lots of distinctions not many differences.

Performance management may often be no more than new wine in old bottles or to mix metaphors a flavor of the month. But it exists and our research demonstrates that interest is growing - Why?

The market economy and entrepreneurial culture of the 1980s focused attention on gaining competitive advantage and getting added value from the better use of resources. Performance orientation became important, especially in the face of global competition and recession. The rise of HRM also contributed to the emergence of performance management. The aims of HRM are:

(*i*) Adopt a strategic approach - one in which HR strategies are integrated with business strategies.

(*ii*) Treat people as assets to be invested into further the interests of the organization.

(*iii*) Obtain higher levels of contribution from people by HRD and reward management.

(*iv*) Gain the commitment of employees to the objectives and values of the organization.

(*v*) Develop a strong corporate culture expressed in mission and value statements and reinforced by communication.

Advocates of performance management believe that it is a practical approach to the achievement of each of these aims. The use of performance management in the best practice companies is not because it is a better technique than performance appraisal, but because it can form one of a number of integrated approaches to the management of performance. The appeal of performance management in its fully realized form is that it is holistic: it pervades every aspect of running the business and helps to give purpose and meaning to those involved in achieving organizational success. The history of performance appraisal from Fowler 1 990, explained in Table 2.1.

Performance Appraisal in India

No one knows precisely when formal methods of reviewing performance were first introduced. According to Koontz (1971), the emperors of the Wei dynasty (AD 221-265) in China had an "Imperial Rater" whose task was to evaluate the performance of the official family. Centuries later, Ignatius Loyola (1491-1556) established a system for formal rating of the members of the Society of Jesus (the Jesuits).

Table 2.1 Management by Objectives, Performance Appraisal and Performance Management Compared

Management by objectives	Performance appraisal	Performance management
Packaged system	Usually tailor made	Tailor made
Applied to managers	Applied to all staff	Applied to all staff
Emphasis on individual objectives	Individual objectives may be included	Emphasis on integrating corporate, team and individual objectives
Emphasis on quantified performance measures	Some qualitative performance indicators may also be included	Competence requirements often included as well as quantified measures
Annual appraisal	Annual appraisal	Continuous review with one or more formal reviews
Top-down system, with ratings	Top-down system, with ratings	Joint process, ratings less common
May not be direct link to pay	Often linked to pay	May not be a direct link to pay
Monolithic system	Monolithic system	Flexible process
Complex paper work	Complex paper work	Documentation often minimized
Owned by line managers and personnel department	Owned by personnel department	Owned by line management

The first formal monitoring systems, however evolved out of the work of Fredrick Taylor and his followers before World War I. Rating for officers in the US Armed Service was introduced in the 1920s and this spread to the UK, as did some the factory based US systems. Merit rating came to the fore in the USA and in UK in the 1950s and 1960s, when it was sometimes rechristened performance appraisal. Management by objectives then came and went in the 1960s and 1970s and, simultaneously, experiments were made with the critical incident technique and behaviourally anchored ratings' scales. A revised form of results-oriented performance appraisal emerged in the 1970s, which still exists today. The term "Performance Management" was first used in the 1970s, but it did not become a recognized process until the latter half of the 1980s.

Merit-rating and Performance Appraisal (Earlier Versions)

WD Scott was the American pioneer who introduced rating of the abilities of workers in industry prior to World War I. He was very much influenced by Taylor and invented the "man to man comparison" scale, which was Taylorism in action (it is possible to argue that many of the developments in this area that followed, even to this day, have been influenced by Taylor). The W D Scott scale was modified and used to rate the efficiency of US army officers. It is said to have supplanted the seniority system of promotion on the basis of merit. The perceived success of this system led to its adoption by the British Army.

The pioneering efforts of Scott were developed in the 1920s and 1930s into what was termed the graphic rating, scale used for reports on workers and for rating managers and supervisors, a typical manager's or supervisor's scale included assessments of various qualities, for example: Consider his success in winning confidence and respect through his personality: inspiring favourable indifferent unfavourable repellent.

Times have changed. The justification made for the use of this sort of rating scale was that they were educational. They ensured, it was said, that those making the reports analyzed subordinates in terms of the traits essential for success in their work. The educational impact on employees was described as imparting knowledge that they were being judged periodically on essential traits considered vital and important. The original scale was said to have been based on thorough research by W D Scott and colleagues into what were the key criteria for rating people at work. But the principle of the scale and the factors used were seized on with enthusiasm by organizations on both sides of the Atlantic as merit rating or, in the 1950s, performance appraisal, flourished. This was without any research into or analysis of the extent to which the factors were relevant. Our survey revealed that some organizations are today using lists of competencies that include items suspiciously like some of the traits identified 70 years or more ago. They seemed to have been lifted down from some shelf without any research into the extent to which they were appropriate in the context of the organization. Merit-rating still exists in some quarters, even if it is now called performance management.

Merit-rating often involved (and still involves under the guise of performance appraisal) the qualification of judgement against each factor, presumably in the belief that the quantification of subjective judgement makes them more objective. Some companies use the total merit sccre as the basis for raking employees, and this is translated into a forced distribution for performance-pay purposes; for example, the top 10 per cent in the ranking get a 5 per cent increase, the next 20 per cent a 4 percent increase, and so on. We heard of one manufacturing company that, to iron out rating inconsistencies, used a diabolical device they called 'factorizing'. An average score was calculated for the whole company and the allocation of point in each department was equated to the company average. Inevitably, line managers objected strongly to the implied assumption that there" were no differences between departmental performances.

Attacks on Merit-rating and Performance Appraisal

Although merit rating in different guises persists, a strong attack on the practice was mounted by McGregor in his highly influential *Harvard Business Review* Article, "An Uneasy Look At Performance Appraisal" (1957). He suggested that the emphasis should be shifted from appraisal to analysis:

This implies a more positive approach. No longer is the subordinate being examined by her superior so that his weakness may be determined; rather he is examining himself, in order to define not only his weakness but also his strength and potentials. He becomes an active agent, not a passive object. He is no longer a Pawn in a chess game called management development.

McGregor went onto propose that the focus should be on the future rather than the past in order to establish realistic targets and to seek the most effective ways of reaching them. The accent of the review is therefore on performance, on actions relative to goals: There is less of a tendency for the personality of the subordinate to become an issue. The superior, instead of finding himself in the position of a psychologist or a therapist, can become a coach helping a subordinate to reach his own decisions on the specific steps that will enable him to reach his targets.

In short, the main factor in the management of performance should be the analysis of the behavior required to achieve agreed results, not the assessment of personality. This is partly management by objectives, which is concerned with planning and measuring results in relation to agreed targets and standards, but retains the concept that performance is about behavior as well as results (a notion that management by objectives ignored).

A mainly forgotten, but still relevant, research project conducted by Rowe (1964) in the UK came to broadly the same conclusion as McGregor-that managers do not like playing at being God in rating the personalities of their subordinates: Managers admitted they were hesitant because what they wrote might be understood, because they might unduly affect a subordinates future career, because they could only write what they were prepared to say and so on.

One comment made to Rowe was that you feel rather like a schoolmaster writing an end-of-term report. Rowe concluded:

- Appraisers were reluctant to appraise.
- The follow-up was inadequate.
- No attempt should be made to clarify or categorised performance in terms of grades. The difficulty of achieving common standards and the reluctance of appraisers to use the whole scale made them of little use.

These comments, especially the last one, are as relevant today as they were more than 30 years ago- and commentators are still producing these percepts as original truths. It is remarkable how much reinventing of the wheel goes on in the field of Performance Management. Another example is the replacement of the discredited management, at least in its earlier versions.

The attack on merit-rating, or on the earlier versions of performance appraisal (as it came to be known in the 1950s), was often made on the grounds that it was mainly concerned with the assessment of traits. These could refer to the extent to which individuals were conscientious, imaginative, self-sufficient, co-operative, or possessed qualities of judgment, initiative, vigour or original thinking. Traits represent predispositions to behave in certain ways in a variety of different situations (Chell 1992). Trait theorists typically advance the following definition of personality: more or less stable internal factors that make one person's behavior consistent from one time to another and different from the behavior other people would manifest in comparable situations' (Hampson 1982). But the belief that trait behavior is independent of situations and the people with whom an individual is interacting is questionable. Trait measure cannot predict how a person will respond in a particular situation (Epstein and O'Brein 1985). And there is the problem of how anyone can be certain that someone has such-and-such a trait. Assessments of traits are only too likely to be prompted by subjective judgements and prejudices.

Management by Objectives

The management by objectives movement claimed that it overcame the problems of trait rating.

Background

The term was first coined by Peter Drucker (1995), when he wrote: What the business enterprise needs a principal of management that will give full scope to individual strength and responsibility and at the same time give common direction of vision and effort, establish teamwork and harmonies the goals of the individual with the common will. The only principal that can do this is management by objectives and self-control.

Drucker emphasized that "an effective management must direct the vision and efforts of all managers towards a common goal". This would ensure that individual and corporate objectives were integrated and also make it possible for managers to control their own performance: Self Control means stronger motivation: a desire to do the best rather than just enough to get by. It means higher performance goal and broader vision.

The Management by Objectives System

Management by objectives was defined by John Humble (1972), a leading British enthusiast, as:

A dynamic system which seeks to integrate the company's need to clarify and achieve its profit and growth goals with the manager's need to contribute and develop himself. It is a demanding and rewarding style of managing a business.

He described management by objectives as a continuous process of:

- Reviewing critically and restarting the company's strategic and tactical plans.
- Clarifying with each manager the key results and performance standards he must achieve and gaining his contribution and commitment to these, individually and as a team member.
- Agreeing with each manager a job improvement plan which makes a measurable and realistic contribution to the unit and company plans for better performance.
- Providing conditions (an organization structure and management information) in which it is possible to achieve the key results and improvement plan.
- Using systematic performance review to measure and discuss progress towards results.
- Developing management training plans to build on strengths, to help managers to overcome their weakness and to get them to accept responsibility for self-development.

- Strengthening the motivation of managers by effective selection, salary and success plans.

Humble emphasized that these techniques are independent and illustrated the dynamic nature of the system as shown in Diagram 2.1.

Fig. 2.1 The Management-by-objectives Cycle

Except for the insistence that this system is exclusively for managers, much of what Humble wrote would be acceptable today as good, if not necessarily best, performance management practice. But management by objectives had become thoroughly discredited by the end of the 1970s why?

Criticisms of Management by Objectives

One of the first and most formidable, attacks on management by objectives was made in the *Harvard Business Review* by Levinson, (1970). His criticisms were as follows:

- Every organization is a social system, a network of interpersonal relationships. A person doing an excellent job by objective standards of measurement may fail miserable as a partner, superior, subordinate or colleague.
- The greater the emphasis on measurement and quantification, the more likely the subtle, non-measurable elements of the task will be sacrificed. Quality of performance frequently loses out to quantification.
- It leaves out the individual's personal needs and objectives, bearing in mind that the most powerful driving force for individuals comprises their needs, wishes and personal objectives.

Another critic writing in the *Havard Business Review* (a favourite medium for attacks on performance appraisal) was Schaffer (1991), who wrote:

Ironically, management by objectives programmes often create heavy paper snowstorms in which managers can escape from demand making. In many MBO programmes, as lists of goods get longer and thicker, the focus is diffused, bulk is confused with quality and energy is spent on the mechanics rather than the results. A manager challenged on the performance of her (*sic*) group can safely point to the packet of papers and assert: 'My managers have spent many hours developing their goals for the year'.

The cause of the demise of management by objectives was no doubt the fact that process became over systematized (often under the influence of package-oriented management consultants) and that too much emphasized was placed on the quantification of objectives. The originator of the concept may not have advocated lots of forms, and they recognized, as John Humble had, that qualitative performance standards could be included in the system, by which was meant a statement of conditions which exist when the result is being satisfactorily achieved. But these principles were often ignored in practice. In addition management by objectives often became a top-down affair with little dialogue and it tended to focus narrowly on the objectives of individual managers without relating them to corporate goals. The system also tended to concentrate on managers, leaving the rest of the staff to be dealt with by an old fashioned merit rating scheme, presumably because it was thought that they did not deserve anything better.

A later comparison of management by objectives performance management by Fowler (1990) criticized the former because:

- It was not right for all Organization—it required a highly structured, orderly and logical approach which did not fit the opportunistic world of the entrepreneur.
- Only limited recognition was given to the importance of defining the organization's corporate goals and

values the emphasis was on the role of the individual manager.

- Line managers perceived it as a centrally imposed administrative task.
- It became a formal once-a-year exercise bearing little relationship to managers' day-to-day activities.
- There was overemphasis on quantifiable objectives to the detriment of important qualitative factors.
- The system was administratively top-heavy-form-filling became an end in itself.

Critical-incident Technique

Critical-incident technique was developed by Flanagan (1954). On the basis of his research, he came to the conclusion that, to avoid trait assessment (merit-rating) and over concentration on output (management by objectives), appraisers should focus on critical behavior incidents which were real unambiguous and illustrated quite clearly how well individuals were performing their tasks. Flanagan advocated that managers should keep a record of these incidents and use them as evidence of actual behavior during review meetings, thus increasing objectivity. He defended this proposal against the suggestion that he was asking managers to keep 'black books ' on the ground that it was positive as well as negative examples that should be recorded, and that it would be better to make a note at the time rather than rely on memory, which is selective and may recall only recent events.

The critical incident technique did not gain much acceptance, perhaps because the 'black book' accusations stuck, but also because it seems to be time consuming. In addition, the problem was raised of converting the incident reports into an overall rating.

But the concept of critical incident has had considerable influence on methods of developing competence frameworks, where it is used to elicit data about effective or less effective behavior. The technique is used to assess what constitutes good or poor performance by analyzing events observed to have a noticeably successful or unsuccessful outcome, thus providing more factual, real information then by simply listing tasks and guessing performance requirements. Used in this way the critical-incident technique produces schedules of 'differentiating competencies' which can form the basis for assessing and, if desired, rating competency levels.

Even if the Flanagan concept of critical incidents has not survived as a specific assessment technique, it does survive as the basis for review processes that rely on factual evidence rather than opinion. The critical incident method can also be used to develop behaviorally anchored rating scales, as described below.

Behaviourally Anchored Ratings Scales

Behaviourally anchored ratings scales are designed to reduce the rating errors that it was assumed are typical of conventional scales. They include a number of performance dimensions such as teamwork, and managers rate each dimension on a scale, as in the following example:

- Continually contributes new ideas and suggestions. Takes a leading role in group meetings but is tolerant and supportive of colleagues and respects other people's points of view. Keeps everyone informed about own activities and is well aware of what other team members are doing in support of team objectives.
- Takes a full part in group meetings and contributes useful ideas frequently. Listens to colleagues and keeps them reasonably well informed about own activities, while keeping abreast of what they are doing.
- Delivers opinions and suggestions at group meetings from time to time, but is not a major contributor to new thinking or planning activities. Generally receptive to other people's ideas and willing to change own plans to fit in. does not always keep others properly informed or take sufficient pains to know what they are doing.
- Tendency to comply passively with other people's suggestions. May be withdrawn at group meetings but

sometimes shows personal antagonism to others. Not very interested in what others are doing or keeping them informed.

- Tendency to go own way without taking much account of the need to make a contribution to team activities. Sometimes uncooperative and unwilling to share information.
- Generally uncooperative. Goes own way, completely ignoring the wishes of other team members and taking no interest in the achievement of team objectives.

It believed that the behavioural descriptions in such scales discourage the tendency to rate on the basis of generalized assumptions about personality traits (which were probably highly subjective) by focusing attention on specific work behaviours. But there is still room for making subjective judgements based on different interpretations subjective judgements based on different interpretations of the definitions of levels of behaviour.

Behaviourally anchored rating scales take time and trouble to develop and are not in common use, except in a modified form as the dimensions in a differentiating competency framework. It is this application that has spread into some performance-management processes.

Performance Appraisal (1970s Version)

In the 1970s a revised approach to performance appraisal was developed under the influence of the management-by-objectives movement. It was sometimes called 'result oriented appraisal' because it incorporated the agreement of objectives and assessment of the results obtained against these objectives. Ratings were usually retained of overall performance and in relation to individual objectives. Trait ratings were also used but, more recently; these have been replaced in some schemes with competence ratings. This form of performance appraisal received a boost during the late 1980s because of the use of performance-related pay based on performance ratings.

Appraisals, as defined by ACAS (1988), regularly record an assessment of an employee's performance, potential and development needs. The appraisal is an opportunity to take an overall view of work content, loads and volume, to look back at what has been achieved during the reporting period and agrees objectives for the next. Appraisal schemes often included ratings of performance factors such as volume of work, quality of work, knowledge of job, dependability, innovation, staff development and communication and an overall rating. Some schemes simply reviewed the achievement of objectives but still included the overall rating. Scope might be allowed for self-assessment, and the forms frequently included spaces for work improvement plans, training requirements and the assessment of potential. There was usually an arrangement for 'counter signing' managers to make comments, generally the appraiser's manager-the appraiser's grandparent'.

In principle many organizations and personnel specialists believed that formal appraisal were desirable. The ACAS (1988) booklet stated that:

Appraisals can help to improve employees' job performanace by identifying stregths and weaknesses and determining how their stregths may be best utilised within the organization and weaknesses overcomes.

But many criticisms were made of the ways in which appraisal schemes operated in practice. Levinson (1976) wrote that it is widely recognized that there are many things wrong with most of the performance appraisal systems in use. He thought that the most obvious drawbacks were that:

- Judgements on performance are usually subjective, impressionistic and arbitrary.
- Ratings by different managers are not comparable.
- Delays in feedback occur, which create frustration when good performance is not quickly recognized and anger when judgement is rendered for inadequacies long past.

- Managers generally have a sense of inadequacy about appraising subordinates and paralysis and procrastination result from feelings of guilt about playing God.

Levinson stated that 'performance appraisal needs to be viewed not as a technique but as a process involving both people and data, and as such the whole process is inadequate. He also pointed out that appraisal was not usually recognized as a normal process of management and that individual objectives were seldom related to the objectives of the business.

A slightly more balanced comment was made by Long (1986) on the basis of the (then) Institute of Personnel Management's research into performance appraisal:

There is no such thing as the perfect performance review system. None are infallible, although some are more fallible than others. Some systems, despite flaws, will be managed fairly conscientiously, others despite elegant design, will receive perfunctory attention and ultimately fail. The relative success or failure of performance review, as with any other organizational system, depends on the attitudinal response it arouses.

The requirements for success were indeed demanding. These were stated by Lazer and Wikstrom (1977) as follows.

A 'good' performance appraisal scheme must be job related, reliable, valid for the purpose for which it is being used, standardized in its administration and suited to the organization's culture.

The problem was that performance appraisal was too often perceived as the property of the personnel department. This was where the forms were kept and where decisions were made about performance related pay. Line managers frequently criticized the system as being irrelevant. They felt they had better things to do; at worst, they ignored it and at best, paid lip-service to completing the forms, knowing that they had to make ratings to generate performance pay. Indeed, managers have been known to rate first in accordance with what pay increase individuals should have and then write their comments to justify their marks. In other words, human beings behaved as human beings. Individuals were said to be wary of appraisals and to be as likely to be de-motivated by an appraisal meeting as the opposite.

Perhaps the worst feature of performance appraisal schemes in the 1970s and 1980s was that appraisal was not regarded as a normal and necessary process of management. If ratings were based on a review of the extent to which individual objectives were attained, those objectives were not linked to the objective of the business or department. Appraisal was isolated and therefore irrelevant.

The concept of 'Appraisal: an idea whose time has gone?' was advanced by Fletcher (1993s). He stated that:

> What we are seeing is the demise of the traditional, monolithic appraisal system.... In its place are evolving a number of separate but linked processes applied in different ways according to the needs of staff.

CHAPTER

3 Pay for Performance

Introduction

Traditionally, pay is a function of position or status in the organisation, not performance or contribution to company goals. In fact, traditional compensation plans make little, if any effort to tie pay to performance. Market demand and equity considerations are far more important factors in establishing pay levels. The characteristic of traditional compensation system is that: *(i)* there is no meaningful relationship between performance and pay. Substantial increases in pay come from promotion to a higher paid job, not from higher performance in the current job; *(ii)* there is an expectation of pay increase by everyone and every year regardless of company, group, or individual performance, and the amount of everyone's increase will be about the same.

Pay for Performance

Over a period of years, many companies have introduced a wide range of non-traditional compensation and reward systems intended to provide for employees a finacial stake in improving company's maximum performance. Different types of non-traditional pay and reward systems, in practice are gain-sharing, small group incentives, individual incentives, lump sum payment/bonus, pay-for-knowledge, profit sharing plans, and so on.

All these plans have in common an effort by companies to slow the growth of base pay and to make a portion (perhaps a substantial portion) of each employee's total compensation variable and tied to company-wide, group, or individual performance. This wave of interest in non-traditional systems suggests that compensation practices in most companies will probably be quite different in the future. The growth of non-traditional compensation systems will change all this. In the future, growth in base pay will slow considerably, and base pay will become a much smaller percentage of total compensation. A larger portion of pay will be variable - go up or down based upon individual's, group's, or company's performance.

Relating pay to competencies: People in most organisations have been paid largely according to their job: internal pay relativities have been driven by assessment of job size through some kind of job evaluation process; and external pay market comparisons have been made on a job basis, either by comparing pay rates directly with similar jobs outside or by using evaluated job size based comparisons.

In its simplest form in fixing 'rate for the job', no account is taken of the performance or capability of the person in the job, except that the person must satisfy the requirements of the job to remain in it. The only way to reward high performance or capability is to promote the ir lividual to a bigger, more demanding job. While this simple rate-for-the-job approach persists in some areas, particularly for some manual employees, most businesses have made attempts over the years to take some account of the individual, especially for managerial, professional, technical and clerical work. In some areas, this has led to incremental pay progression, rewarding time spent in the job.

What has changed in recent years and what has led to the growing interest in relating pay to competencies, is the progressive challenging of structuralist view of organisation. Most organisations are changing—not just changing their structures, but also the way in which they are organised. Delayering; team working; project working; flexibility; organising around businesses processes; lateral rather than vertical career development—these are all areas of change for most organisations in today's environment. Together, they challenge the notion of a job defined purely in structural/hierarchical terms, and hence the pay management processes have been built up on this model. In particular, they challenge the traditional separation of 'jobs' and 'people', and the way that these issues have been handled through , separate management processes.

It seems entirely reasonable that the pay of the individual should in some way reflect the skills and competencies which they bring and use and so encourage the development of these skills and competencies. However, it is now widely recognised that paying only for competencies is just as one-sided a view as paying only for jobs. The more recent ventures into relating pay to competencies have taken a more balanced perspective in which it is recognised that pay needs to be related to a number of factors, including the role; the skills and competencies of the individual; the performance and results achieved; and the market. The real issue is how to achieve the best balance between these factors to meet particular business requirements and circumstances. If this balance is achieved, then relating pay to competencies can have a powerful and positive impact, by rewarding and encouraging the behaviour which the organisation needs for its success.

To get the best balance between the various factors which may determine pay, the basic question arises what do we want to pay people for? Overall levels of pay will be influenced by the external market, and the organisation's require relationship to that market, given its business performance and its overall plans and strategies. In principle, people are paid for the job or role they carry out (as in the traditional model); for their capability (i.e., the skills and competencies which they bring); or for the performance they achieve.

There are two general ways in which pay may be related to competencies. The first is by building competencies into the performance management process, and then relating pay movement through a pay range to access performance. The second and more explicit way of relating pay to competencies is through the use of role profiling or job family approach. This is particularly useful in managing pay progression through the wider pay bands associated with the move to fewer grades, or broadbands. In principle, these two approaches are fundamentally the same. In both cases, individuals (rather than jobs) are being assessed against defined criteria - skills, competencies and contribution and positioned into the pay structure accordingly. The difference is largely about presentation: in the first case it is presented as a grade structure, while in the second it is presented as a pattern of pay zones within a broadbanded arrangement.

Financial Incentives

An 'incentive' or 'reward* can be anything that attracts a worker's attention and stimulates him to work. In the words of Burack and Smith, "An incentive scheme is a plan or programme to motivate individual or group performance. An incentive programme is most frequently built on monetary rewards (incentive pay or monetary bonus), but may also include a variety of non-monetary rewards or prizes."

The concept of incentive implies increased willingness or motivation to work and not the capacity to work. It refers to all the plans that provide extra pay for extra performance in addition to regular wages for a job. Under this programme, the income of an individual, a small group, a plant workforce or all the employees of a firm are partially or wholly related to some measure of productive output. Wage incentives are extra financial motivation. They are designed to stimulate human effort by rewarding the person, over and above the time rated remuneration, for improvements in the present or targeted results. Basically, the wage incentive implies a system of payment under which the amount payable to a person is linked with his output. Such a payment may also be called payment by results.

Determinants of Incentives

The effective use of incentives depends on three variables—the individual, work situation and incentive plan.

The individual: Different people value things differently. Enlightened managers realise that all people do not attach the same value to monetary incentives, bonuses, prizes or tips. Employees view these things differently because of age, marital status, economic need and future objectives.

The work situation: This is made up of four important elements:

- *(a) Technology:* The operation of a machine or work system which can establish a range of incentives;
- *(b) Satisfying job assignments:* A worker's job may incorporate a number of activities that he finds satisfying. Incentives may take the form of earned time-off, greater flexibility in hours worked, extended vacation time and other privileges that an individual values;
- *(c) Feedback:* A worker needs to be able to see the connection between his work and rewards. These responses provide important reinforcement; and
- *(d) Equity:* A worker considers fairness or reasonableness as part of the exchange for his work.

Incentive plan: An incentive plan has the following important features:

- *(a)* An incentive plan may consist of both 'monetary' and 'non-monetary' elements. Mixed elements can provide the diversity needed to match the needs of individual employees.
- *(b)* The timing, accuracy and frequency of incentives are the very basis of a successful incentive plan.
- *(c)* The plan requires that it should be properly communicated to the employees to encourage individual performance, provide feedback and encourage redirection.

Classification of Incentives

Incentives may broadly be classified into monetary or non-monetary. Monetary incentives have an important contribution to make within the total motivation pattern. They provide extra-financial motivation, by rewarding the worker over and above his regular remuneration for performing more than the targeted work. Some of the financial motivations are overtime wages, higher basic wages, incentive bonus, merit increments, suggestion rewards, various allowances, promotion and fringe benefits.

Some of the non-financial incentives are good human relations, self-respect, recognition, status, sense of belonging, appreciation, higher responsibility, greater authority, job satisfaction, improved working conditions and greater leisure. AH these motivate workers to raise their productivity.

Monetary incentives imply external motivation, non-monetary incentives involve internal motivation. Both are important. It is a judicious mix-up of the two that tends to cement incentives with motivation.

Rewards or incentives may also be classified into direct compensation and indirect compensation.

Direct compensation includes the basic salary or wage that the individual is entitled to for his job, overtime-work and holiday premium, bonuses based on performance, profit sharing and opportunities to purchase stock options and so on.

Indirect compensation includes protection programmes (insurance plans, pensions), pay for time not worked, services and perquisites. But these are maintenance factors rather than reward components. Since they are made available to all employees, irrespective of performance, they will tend to retain people in the organisation but not stimulate them to greater effort and higher performance.

Sometimes, the rewards are also termed as intrinsic rewards and extrinsic rewards. The former are those that an individual receives for himself. They are largely a result of the job that the worker does. The techniques of job enrichment, shorter work weeks, flexible work hours, project structures and job rotation can offer intrinsic rewards through providing interesting and challenging jobs and allowing the worker greater freedom. On the other hand, the latter rewards refer to direct compensation, indirect compensation and non-financial rewards.

Incentives have also been classified into individual, group and organisation-wide:

Individual incentives: One of the major proponents of individual incentives was Frederick Taylor. There are certain characteristics of individual incentives. First, they are not applicable to many jobs, such as those with no physical output measure of performance or those where individual contributions are difficult to assess. Second, individual incentives can cause a wide range of administrative problems. These include *(a)* the cost of time study to set and keep current production standards for multiple jobs, *(b)* the cost of tracking output in these multiple jobs and calculating payments, and *(c)* the difficulty in setting production standards that are accepted as appropriate by both management and workers. Individual incentives are most likely to work when there is trust in management and where production standards do not undergo regular change.

In an individual incentive plan, the rewards of incentives are based solely on individual performance. It is the extra compensation paid to an individual over a specified amount for his production effort. Such a system is feasible only where an individual can increase the quantity and quality of his output by his own individual efforts and where his output can be measured. The paymment is normally on a monthly basis, though in a few cases it may be quarterly or other convenient periods. The standards of performance have been set by a qualified industrial engineering analyst, using technically sound work measurement procedures. The rewards under this plan are almost always immediate, that is, paid daily or weekly.

The advantages of individual wage incentive plans are relatively obvious and straight forward. First and foremost, the individual incentive plan rewards the individual for his or her production. The more the worker produces, the more the worker earns. Second, the individual incentives appeal to the basic need for money found in most people. Almost everyone will work harder, up to a point, when there is a justifiable reason to believe that increased productivity will bring about a personal gain.

Although individual wage incentives have advantages, there are also limitations. Individual wage incentives work best with jobs that are primarily operator-controlled. They may also lead to labour problems. Incentives, because they reward production levels, can lead to quality problems. Safeguards must be taken to ensure that quality is not sacrificed for quantity. It is the output of the group rather than that of each individual member of the group that can be measured most conveniently or accurately.

Group incentives: Profit sharing is better known, older and more widely practiced than gain sharing. Profit sharing is associated with participative management theories. Profit sharing is a group-based organisation plan. The logic behind profit sharing seems to be twofold. First, it is seen as a way to encourage employees to think more like owners or atleast be concerned with the success of the organisation as a whole. Individual oriented plans often place little emphasis on these broader goals. Second, it permits labour costs to vary with the organisation's ability to pay.

Some companies have effectively used their profit sharing plans as vehicles for educating employees about the financial performance of the business. The most important advantage of profit sharing is that it makes labour costs of an organisation variable and adjust them to the organisation's ability to pay. Most Japanese firms have used this approach to adjusting labour costs for decades. Group or area incentive schemes provide for the payment of a bonus either equally or proportionately to individuals within a group or area. The bonus is related to the output achieved over an agreed standard or to the time saved on the job - the difference between allowed time and actual time. Such schemes may be most appropriate where:

(*a*) people have to work together and teamwork has to be encouraged; and

(*b*) high levels of production depend a great deal on the co-operation existing among a team of workers as compared with the individual efforts of team members.

Group bonuses are calculated on the basis of the output of the team and are divided among the members either equally or in specified proportions, with more being given to skilled employees than to those who are unskilled. Group incentives are usually applied to small teams and the rewards are based on the performance of the entire group. The bonuses are often much larger than individual wage incentives.

Group incentive plans since they evaluate overall performance, are applicable to a wide variety of tasks. Sometimes, however, they are applied to all workers of a 'department or even of a whole undertaking. One of the disadvantages of group incentive plan is that there is a possibility of ignoring the individual performance as the rewards are based on group performance. In large groups it is often inevitable that there will be slackers who can disrupt the functioning of the whole group.

Organisation-wide incentives: The organisation-wide incentive system involves co-operation and collective effort of the employees and management in order to accomplish broader organisational objectives, such as:

(i) to reduce labour, material and supply costs;

(ii) to decrease turnover and absenteeism;

(iii) to strengthen employee loyalty to the company; and

(iv) to promote harmonious labour management relations.

One of the aspects of the organisation-wide incentive scheme is profit-sharing under which an employee receives a share of the profit fixed in advance under an agreement freely entered into. Some of the advantages of such a scheme are:

(i) it inculcates in employees' a sense of economic discipline as regards wage costs and productivity;

(ii) it engenders improved communication and increased sense of participation;

(iii) it is relatively simple and its cost of administration is low; and

(iv) it is non-inflationary, if properly devised.

Wage Incentive Systems

The term 'wage incentive' has been used both in the restrictive sense of participation and in the widest sense of financial motivation. According to Hummel and Nickerson, "it refers to all the plans that provide extra pay for extra performance in addition to regular wages for a job." In the words of National Commission on Labour, "wage incentives are extra financial motivation. They are designed to stimulate human effort by rewarding the person, over and above the time rated remuneration, for improvements in the present targeted results."

Some of the important wage incentive systems are as follows:

The Halsey system: This system which was developed by F.A. Halsey, provides for the fixation of a standard time for the completion of the task. For the work done in correct time or more, the actual time rate is paid. Thus, the minimum age is guaranteed even if the output falls below the standard. If the job is completed on less than the standard time, the worker receives a bonus payment at his time rate for a specific percentage of the time saved. This percentage may vary anywhere from 30 percent to 70 percent, but usually it is fixed at 50 percent (the other 50 percent going to the share of employer). Thus, if a worker does the work in 6 houis against 10 hours standard, he gets bonus after 6 hours plus 50 percent of 4 hours, i.e., 2 hours, as bonus. The other 50 percent (2 hours) is shared by the employer (formula given below).

$$\text{Bonus} = \frac{1}{2} \text{ of } \frac{\text{Time Saved}}{\text{Time Taken}} \times \text{Daily Wage}$$

The Rowan system: Under this system also a standard time is allowed for a job, and bonus is similarly paid for any time saved. This plan differs from the Halsey plan only in regard to the determination of the bonus. In all other respects, the two are the same. The premium is calculated on the basis of the proportion which the time saved bears to standard time. Thus, if a worker does work in 6 hours against the 10-hour standard, the wage payable is 6 hours wages plus 40 percent of the wage as bonus (formula given below).

$$\text{Bonus} = \frac{\text{Time Saved}}{\text{Time Allowed}} \times \text{Time Taken} \times \text{Hourly Rate}$$

The Barth Variable Sharing System: This system is similar to the Halsey and Rowan systems. It is also based on standard time, but does not provide for a guaranteed time rate. The worker's pay is ascertained by multiplying the standard hour by the number of hours actually taken to do the job, taking the square root of the product and multiplying by the worker's hourly rate. This system does not guarantee the worker his time rate for levels of output below standard. Moreover, the worker's earnings under this system are always lower than under straight piecework for standard task, but for low task, higher than under straight piece-work at certain levels of output above standard.

The Bedaux Point System: Under this system, the standard time set is divided into a number of points at the rate of one minute per point. The bonus is calculated at 75 percent of the points earned in excess of 60 per hour. Thus, if the standard time is 10 hours and if the worker completes the job in 7 hours and if his hourly rate is 0.96 money units, the standard number of points for completing the job is (100 points. The worker thus earns 600 points in 7 hours. His bonus, therefore, will be 75 percent of 180 × 0.96/60 which is equal to 2.16 money units. If a worker does not reach the standard, he is paid at his time rate. This system is really more than the incentive system, since it enables the management to record the output of any worker of the department in units which show at once if the production is upto the standard the management desires.

In spite of certain advantages, especially its applicability to a large variety of jobs in the plant, the Bedaux system has been severely criticised because of *(i)* the expense of installation and administration; *(ii)* difficulties in explaining it to workers; *(iii)* the returns to the workers in the way of increased earnings do not purportedly commensurate with the increase in production.

The taylor differential piece rate system: This system was introduced by Taylor with two objects. First, to give sufficient incentive to workmen to induce them to produce up to their full capacity and second, to remove the fear of wage cut. There is one rate for those who reach the standard; they are given a higher rate to enable them to get the bonus. The other is the lower rate for those who are below the standard, so that the hope of receiving a higher rate may serve as an incentive come upto the standard. Workers are expected to do certain units of work within a certain period of time. This standard is determined on the basis of time and motion studies. Such scientific determination assumes that the standard fixed is not unduly high and is within the easy reach of workers. On a proper determination of the standard depends the success of the scheme. This system is designed to encourage the specially efficient worker with a higher rate of payment and to penalise the inefficient by a lower rate of payment. In practice, this plan is seldom used now.

Premium and task bonuses: It has been devised by H.L. Gantt and is the only one that pays a bonus percentage multiplied by the standard time. Under this system, fixed time rate are guaranteed. Output standards and time standards are established for the performance of each job. Workers completing the job within the standard time or in less time receive wages for the standard time plus a bonus which ranges from 20 percent to 50 percent of the time allowed and not time saved. When a worker fails to turn out the required quantity of a product, he simply gets his time rate without any bonus. Its fairness and practical value depends on the reasonableness of the standard fixed and the wages which workers of average ability can earn without having to work at excessive speed and becoming unduly fatigued.

The profit sharing system: The profit sharing scheme is based on the same principle as the group system where incentive is related to the collective effort of the group. It is an arrangement freely entered into under which an employer gives to his employees a share in the net profits of the enterprise, fixed in advance, in addition to their wages. The essential features of profit sharing scheme are:

(*a*) that the management is voluntary but based on an agreement between employer and employee;

(*b*) that the amount to be distributed amongst the participants depena upon the profits earned by the enterprise; and

(*c*) that the proportion of the profits to be distributed is determined well in advance.

The aims of profit sharing plans are:

(*a*) to promote increased effort and ouput;

(*b*) to share some gains in the productivity of the firm;

(*c*) to secure employee co-operation and to achieve industrial harmony; and

(*d*) to strengthen unity of interest and employee loyalty to organisation objectives.

The profit sharing scheme is comparatively easy and less expensive to adopt. In some cases, these schemes have become successful resulting in increased production at a lower cost. There are cases where they have not made any significant contribution towards improving the overall efficiency of the company. To be effective, profit-sharing schemes should be based on the considerations of profitability of industrial units, computation of surplus profit for distribution on an average basis and fair return on capital invested in an enterprise. It should not be treated as a substitute for adequate wages but provide something extra to the participants. Full support and co-operation of the union is to be obtained in implementing such a scheme.

The scanlon plan: It is a plant-wide incentive scheme developed by Joseph Scanlon of the United Steelworkers of America in 1927. The basic concept underlying the Scanlon Plan is that efficiency depends upon plant-wide co-operation. The purpose of this incentive plan is to develop teamwork. It has two main aspects:

(*a*) adopting a measure for increased productivity; and

(*b*) sharing the gain accrued from that increased productivity. The objective of the plan is to devise a formula, which will most adequately reflect the prospective efforts of workers and management as a whole. The bonus formula is devised to fit the particular operating conditions of the plant.

If there are serious irrationalities in the *pay* packet or wage structure, they should be corrected before the scheme is actually introduced.

The incentive earnings should be sufficiently generous to convince employees that they are being adequately paid for their extra effort.

The basis for sharing gains of productivity should be fair to employees and are to be worked out in agreement with unions.

A periodic review of the working of the scheme should be undertaken if the scheme is to retain its dynamic character and with a view to applying timely correctives.

If expertise for designing and implementing the incentive scheme is not available in an organisation, advice and assistance of an outside expert or a consultant should be taken. An incentive scheme, if not properly worked out and implemented, can do more harm than good.

If the choice for increasing production lies between the system of overtime and incentive bonus, the latter should be preferred. Overtime induces workmen to earn more by slackening their pace of work during the scheduled hours. Thus, it represents a form of disguised unemployment.

Incentives are not to be used to induce workers to work so fast that they are unduly fatigued and their health suffers.

For effective implementation of incentive plans:

1. Link the incentive with the company's strategy.
2. Ensure that effort and rewards are directly related.
3. Make the plan understandable and calculable by the employees.
4. Set effective standards.

5. Guarantee the standards.
6. Guarantee an hourly base rate.
7. Get support for the plan.
8. Develop good measurement systems.
9. Emphasise long-term as well as short-term success.
10. Take the corporate culture into consideration.

Some of the salient features of the plan are:

(a) it encourages group work;

(b) there is high flexibility in the generation of decisions and execution of the plan;

(c) it integrates the company's objectives with group activity;

(d) it involves all the workers in the exercise and they make their maximum personal contribution to the process of production.

Earnest Dale has described four degrees of co-operation between labour and management in the Scan Ion Plan, namely;

(a) information cooperation by gathering information;

(b) advisory co-operation through the process of consultation;

(c) constructive co-operation by making suggestions for improvement; and

(d) joint union-management decision making.

The rucker plan: The philosophy of the Rueker Plan is similar to the Scanlon Plan, but the bonus computed is based on a more sophisticated basis. There are two major differences between the two plans. The standard under the Rucker Plan is based upon a careful study of accounting records and is not considered bargainable. While the Scanlon Plan rewards only savings in labour costs, the Rucker Plan offers incentives for savings in other areas as well.

Under the Rucker Plan, the objective of the management is not the enlargement of the production volume, but the enlargement of value added. The Rucker Plan is worked out on the basis that whenever there is an increase in value added, a fixed percentage of that increase should be paid out to employees in the form of a bonus since they have contributed to that increase. According to Rucker, value added is the production value created by the company or the plant, as a result of using raw materials and other inputs. This production value so created should be shared among the parties who have contributed towards its creation, *viz.*, employees (who contributed labour), shareholders (who contributed assets and capital) and government (which contributed infrastructure).

Merit rating: Mention may be made of merit rating as a form of wage incentive. It presupposes that the workers in a given grade or occupation differ in their efficiency at work in the undertaking. Merit rating is a method of attempting to give recognition to the best workers by systematic objective standards. Various qualities are listed, such as skill, efficiency, reliability, initiative, care in avoiding accidents, adaptability, co-operation with other workers and regularity of attendance. Points or gradings are given for each of these qualities and workers who reach a high level receive an addition to the normal rate of pay for the job. Rating may be done for each year and workers who had been receiving merit pay.

SECTION-B

CHAPTER

4 Collective Bargaining

Introduction

In this chapter, we will discuss the interaction between workers' union, employers' organization and the state for the purpose of rule making, which is what collective bargaining is all about. The concept and nature of collective bargaining and the two key ILO conventions—Convention No. 87 on freedom of association and Convention No. 98 on the right to collective bargaining—are briefly discussed. The legal framework for collective bargaining is explained with special regard to recognition/determination of collective bargaining agent/council. This chapter examines the distinction between settlement, agreement, and award; the distinction between collective and individual agreement; and the differences between rights and interest issues. Thereafter, the legal position in India with regard to the right to bargain and unfair labour practices of both emploeyrs and unions are discussed.

This chapter examines the various levels at which collective bargaining takes place, the duration and the content/substance of collective bargaining agreements in India (also their implications for management). It also covers the key negotiation techniques and skills, the conditions for mutual gains bargaining, and the care that needs to be exercised while drafting an agreement. The critical thinking and role-play exercise focus on the 'how' part of the subject.

The Concept

The term 'collective bargaining' extends to all negotiations that take place between an employer, a group of employers, or one or more employers' organizations, on the one hand and one or more organizations, on the other to:

(*a*) determine the working conditions and terms of employment; and/or

(*b*) regulate relations between employers and workers; and/or

(*c*) regulate relations between employers or their organizations and a workers' organization or workers' organizations.

Collective bargaining is a method by which trade unions protect, safeguard and improve the conditions of their members' working lives. The participants in the process are employers or their organizations and worker representatives, usually trade unions. The government is sometimes involved as a third player. Individual bargaining between an employer and his/her employees is not regarded as collective bargaining. That process usually culminates in the conclusion of an agreement, usually known as a 'collective agreement'.

Collective bargaining is a means of joint regulation by employers (alone or through ' their organizations) and workers' organizations. Respect for rules depends on the manner of their formulation. Collective bargaining provided the opportunity to formulate rules by mutual consent.

Some view the process of collective bargaining as one of unions sharing governance with management; this influences regulation or rule making and results in a contract Several analysts have focused on the economic and political functions of collective bargaining: For instance, while some emphasize the economic functions, others highlight the political role of trade unions in collective bargaining. In most cases, the dynamics of economic and political factors and forces together determine the outcomes of collective bargaining.

According to the ILO, freedom of association (Convention No. 87) and collective bargaining (Convention No.98) are fundamental rights. Both freedom of association and the right to collective bargaining form an integral part of the ILO Declaration on Fundamental Principles and Rights at Work, OECD's core labour standards, (WTO's) social clause, and the United Nations' 'Global Compact'. All four refer to the same labour rights.

The Nature of Collective Bargaining

In some countries, it *is* considered the duty of employers to engage in collective bargaining in good faith, in others (for instance, Australia) it is pot. Then there arc countries (for instance, Cyprus and Malaysia) that distinguish between interest issues and rights issues. In these countries, collective bargaining can take place on interest issues and not on rights issues. *Interest issues* refer to wages and working conditions. *Rights issues* concern the interpretation of do's and don'ts in the course of an employment relationship. There is a distinction between market relations and managerial aspects. The former can be a candidate for collective bargaining, not the latter. *Market relations* are concerned with wages and working conditions. *Managerial aspects* have to do with issues like assignment of work and adjustment of workforce. While in some countries, such as India, anything and everything can be bargained for in others, such as Malaysia, hiring, reward, transfer, promotion, assignment of work and adjustment of workforce are explicitly recognized by law as managerial prerogatives.

Freedom of Association and Protection of the Right to Organize Convention, 1948 (No. 87)

Convention No. 87 provides for the right of workers and employers, without any distinction, to establish and join organizations of their own choosing without previous authorization. Their organizations have the right to form or join federations and confederations, including at the international level. These organizations or federations may not be liable to arbitrary dissolution or suspension by an administrative authority. Workers' and employers' organizations have the right to draw up their own constitutions and rules, elect their representatives and organize their activities, without any interference which would restrict this right or prevent its lawful exercise. Rules for the acquisition of legal personality of workers' and employers' organizations may not be of such a character as to restrict the application of the basic right to organize. In exercising the rights provided by the Convention, workers and employers and their organizations must respect the laws of the land applicable to all persons and organizations. However, these laws must not be such as to impair the guarantees provided for in the Conventions, nor may they be applied in such a way. The only exception to the cardinal principle of the right to organize 'without distinction whatsoever' is the armed forces and the police, to whom special rules and regulations may apply.

The Right to Organize and Collective Bargaining Convention, 1949 (No. 98)

This Convention aims to protect the exercise of the right to organize and to promote voluntary collective bargaining.

- Workers must be adequately protected against acts of anti-union discrimination, in particular acts calculated to:
  - make the employment of a worker subject to conditions that he or she does not join a union or gives up trade union membership;
  - cause the dismissal or otherwise prejudice a worker because of trade union membership or participation in trade union activities.
- Both workers' and employers' organizations shall enjoy adequate protection against acts of interference by each other or each other's agents or members, including in particular.
  - acts designed to promote the establishment of workers' organizations under the domination of employers' organizations;

* the provision of financial or other support to workers' organizations for the purpose of placing them under the control of employers or employers' organizations.

- Ratifying states must take measures to encourage and promote the full development and use of machinery for voluntary collective bargaining as regards terms and conditions of employment.

As an Convention no. 87, special provisions may be made for the armed forces and the police. However, unlike Convention no. 87, Convention no. 98 allows for the exclusion from its scope of Public servants engaged in the administration of the State.

Source: www.ilo.org

Collective bargaining provides for procedural and substantial rules. *Procedural rules* concern mechanisms for dealing with interpretations and implementations of agreements as well as resolving conflicts, whereas, *substantial rules* concern the substance of the agreement, in both markets (terms and conditions of employment) and managerial relationships (control on manning, transfers, promotions, etc.).

Collective bargaining is viewed as a process of give and take rather than 'giving in'. However, in many countries, the process tends to promote antagonism and conflict between the parties, because of which collective bargaining takes place in a spirit of barring the gain (to the other party). Therefore, the future of collective bargaining is contingent on its transformation into a cooperative process. Usually, though, cooperative pacts are viewed in some cases as 'suicide pacts'. Trade unions are concerned about the secondary effects of cooperation pacts: by signing cooperation pacts unions are working for the survival of the company, which is essential for workers' jobs and income security. Yet, unions are worried whether in such a situation they remain a union the way workers (or their members) perceived them all along.

With the evolution of industrial and employment relations in the face of rapid changes and significant advances in technology, among other things, collective bargaining became, in some sectors and countries, an instrument of social change. Shifts in the labour and product markets created pressures as well as opportunities for a new approach to collective bargaining. Besides subsistence concerns, collective bargaining started addressing the challenges of jobs, incomes, social security, changes in organizations, skills development and governance, as well as responding to the challenges of occupational safety and environment. In 1984, the ILO documented 400 tripartite and bipartite agreements across 20 OECD countries following the oil price shocks and the resultant recession and structural changes in industrialized market economies of Western Europe and North America, Fifteen years later the ILO commissioned a study in twelve countries in Asia and elsewhere, including developing countries like India, to assess how negotiated changes were helping m ushering flexibility and promoting adaptability at the firm level. A survey of collective bargaining in different countries over different time periods revealed that economic, institutional and political environments have a bearing on the kind of effect that collective bargaining has on die economic performance of firms and the well being of workers. Important complementarities exist between key aspects of the bargaining system. Therefore, the impact of individual aspects such as union density or centralization of bargaining cannot be assessed in isolation. It is the package of institutions that matter.

Contrary to popular misconception, neither labour nor labour laws are the real problem behind India's lacklustre performance in industry. India has been leveraging for long on very cheap labour. Even though the proportionate costs of labour have been declining, these are still high due to low productivity. However, low labour productivity is not just a function of labour: the Asian Development Bank noted that poor and weak social and physical infrastructure has been the bane of India.

Labelled the 'labour aristocracy' (Rannadive 1990), a growing proportion of the working class in the organized sector, which enjoys the right to collective bargaining, is white collared with middle-class aspirations and standards of living. Human resource managers, trade unions and employees have begun to realize that their future is as secure as that of the organization they work in. The pressure of competition is making people understand the need to take a holistic view of business: people, technology, environment, structures, systems, processes, etc. Workers and unions are realizing that in reality it is the customer, not the employer who ultimately guarantees their job, income and well-being. Employers/managements and unions/workers are acting together to make their firms competitive, and to save the maximum number of jobs, if necessary with a variety of tradeoffs. People in traditional societies generally more comfortable with pattern maintenance, are now also seeing the imperatives of adaptation. They also understand the consequences of not only doing things differently, but also of not adapting to changes in the environment as well.

Negotiated changes in response to economic liberalization and enterprise restructuring mean, for most workers, accepting workforce reductions, job wage tradeoffs and die consequential reorganiza-tion of work. This in turn is leading to doing different things (multi-skiffing) in different ways (flexibility). However, the real challenge that collective bargaining is still to address is: How and how soon can the emphasis be shifted from the current cost-cutting approach to value creation and value addition.

Collective bargaining has undergone changes at different time periods. Even when the initial notion of acquired interests, based on the assumption that employment—like land or capital—is an asset, gained currency wage rates were influenced in economic terms more by the laws of supply and demand and in political terms by the relative balance of power. Subsequently, with the emergence of the concept of the welfare state and of communist ideology, employment conditions started being determined not only by supply and demand and balance of power, but also by moral notions of the minimum standard of living. In the wake of the rise of market forces, there has been a shift in wage fixation from 'to each according to his need', to 'to each according to his or her skill, effort, responsibility, and working conditions'. The ILO Convention on Equal Remuneration for Work of Equal Value was founded on this criterion. The ILO's Declaration on fundamental Principles and Rights at work and their Follow-up underlines the need for member countries to respect collective bargaining and end discrimination in employment and remuneration.

In the context of globalization, the changes in collective bargaining can be viewed from the social, political, and economic points of view. Sociologically, the trend towards individual contracts reflects the difficulties in the mobilization of the working class due to pay differentiation across skills and competitive forces undermining lateral trust among workers. With die diversification in economic activities and the diminishing contribution from traditional sources, the homogeneity of manual workers and the power of trade unions—what was structured around manual and clerical jobs in the organized sector—have been on the decline. Politically, wage developments reflect the tradeoff between pay and control over jobs. A study of the newspaper industry points out that though workers' real wages improved (due, of course, more to the efforts of working and non-working journalists' wage boards than collective bargaining), control over work shifted from management to employers, which was due to technological changes. Bank chairmen openly assert that if bank employees exit industry settlements some of them can pay more than what they are presendy earning. Employers and managements who consider unions a problem are sending signals to workers that they would get a higher pay if they allow them to decide unilateraHy than they would through bargaining collectively. During the 1970s and 1980s, trade unions bargained for higher wages for their members. Often, this had either the intended or the unintended effect of securing higher wages for permanent workers at the expense of temporary, casual, contract and contingent workers. During the late 1980s and 1990s when the enterprise level's permanent workforce began to shrink rapidly and the casual, contract, or contingent workforce began to increase, trade unions realized that their future membership base would lie more in the latter category. During the late 1990s, thus, trade unions began to press for non-discrimination in remuneration between temporary and contract workers. Since the 1980s, trade unions of many companies have collaborated with managements in introducing two-track production (old and new greenfield sites) and two-tier wage systems (recently recruited workers and workers employed in new plants getting less wages than older workers). Trade unions are now aware of the need to taper off the wage differentials.

The Legal Framework of Collective Bargaining

Article 19(c) of the Constitution of India guarantees freedom of association as a fundamental right. This was recognized in the Trade Unions Act, 1926, Industrial Disputes Act, 1947, and the Industrial Employment (Standing Orders) Act, 1946. In 1923, India ratified ILO Convendon No. 11 concerning the Right of Association for Agricultural Workers. It has, however, not ratified ILO Convention Nos. 87 and 98 due to 'technical difficulties' involving trade union rights for civil servants. This is not a valid reason for non-ratification, because a ratifying country can exempt certain services. The real intention could be to restrict freedom of association to only manual workers (by defining them as workers) and exclude supervisory and managerial workers. The government does not to allow the right of collective bargaining to industrial workers in Government undertakings, such as the railways, posts, telecommunications, and the Central Public Works Department. Remuneration, etc. is decided by the government on the basis of Pay Commission recommendations and not through collective bargaining. The labour laws at the national level do not mandate employers either to recognize unions or to engage in collective bargaining. However, some states (for instance, Andhra Pradesh, Bihar, Gujarat, Karnataka, Madhya Pradesh, Maharashtra, Orissa and West Bengal) have provisions concerning recognition of trade unions.

Determining Collective Bargaining Agent

From 1931 to date, the identification of a collective bargaining agent has remained a hotly debated issue. The Royal Commission on Labour (India 1931) was not in favour of the idea that recognition should depend on the numerical strength of die union. If a union consisted of only a minority of employees, it was not adequate reason for withholding recognition. The 1947 amendment to the Trade Unions Act, 1926 and the Trade Union Bill, 1950, provided for recognition of more than one union by an employer, though neither was passed by the Parliament. In 1956 the Second Five Year Plan stressed the importance of one union, in one industry. In 1958, the Indian Labour Conference evolved a code of discipline in industry—which did not and still does not have statutory force—which contained criteria for recognition of unions. It was in favour of workers belonging to non-recognized unions operating through the representative union of the industry or seeking redressal of grievances directly. The First National Commission on Labour (India 1969) left the matter of union recognition to be decided on the basis of local circumstances. The Second National Commission on Labour (India 2002) has made specific recommendations on this issue.

There is no law at the national level for recognition of trade unions. However, in some states—Maharashtra and Madhya Pradesh, for instance—there are legal provisions for it. Thus, in India, there are a number of ways of determining a representative union for the purposes of collective bargaining. These methods include (*a*) Code of Discipline, which is common across most public sector undertakings; (*b*) secret ballot, which is mandatory in three states, namely, Andhra Pradesh (since 1975), Orissa (since 1994) and West Bengal (since 1998); (*c*) check-off system, which is favoured by some unions; and (*d*) membership verification. In 1995, the Supreme Court of India directed a government corporation, the Food Corporation of India, to resolve the trade union recognition dispute through secret ballot. The judgment also mandated die procedure for the secret ballot. In 1982, the Bombay High Court struck down an order of the industrial court for a secret ballot in the case of Maharashtra General Karngar Union v. Bayer India Ltd. The matter was taken to die division bench of the High Court, which upheld die order of the single judge. What had to be proved by the Maharashtra General Karngar Union was that the membership of the Mazdoor Congress had fallen to less than 30% during the requiske six-month period. It was argued that hypothetically, if 25 of 100 workers in an establishment voted for a recognized union, it meant that the membership had fallen below the requisite percentage but, in the absence of the identity of the voters, it would not be possible to prove that the union members had voted against it,

Under Section 2(p) of the Industrial Disputes Act, 1947, collective agreements to settle disputes can be reached with or without recourse to the conciliation machinery-established by legislation. An *agreement* with one trade union is not binding on members of another or other union(s) unless arrived at during conciliation proceedings; the Other union(s)—including a minority union—can, therefore, raise an industrial dispute. Under Section 36 (1) of the Industrial Disputes Act, which deals with workers' representation, a collective agreement is binding on the workers who have negotiated and individually signed the settlement. It is not binding on workers who do not sign the settlement or authorize any other worker to sign on their behalf.

However, a *settlement* (a written agreement between employer and workers), arrived at in the course of conciliation proceedings is binding, under Section 18(3) of the Act, not only on die actual parties to the industrial dispute but also on the heirs, successors, or assignees of the employer on the one hand

and all the workers m the establishment—present or future—on the other.

When parties fail to reach an agreement or settlement and the matter is referred for arbitration or adjudication, the award of the arbitrator or adjudicator is binding on the parties concerned.

An 'award' means an interim or a final determination of any industrial dispute or of any question relating thereto by any Labour Court, Industrial Tribunal, National Industrial Tribunal and includes an arbitration award made under section 10A. They are enforceable under Section 33 (c) by the labour court or 17(B) of the Industrial Disputes Act after the expiry of 30 days from the date of publication in the official gazette. If an award is not honoured by either of the parties, the party which is guilty of not honouring can be prosecuted against under Section 29 of the Industrial Disputes Act. The penalty for not honouring an award could be six months imprisonment or fine. The powers under Section 29 of the Industrial Disputes Act are not vested in labour courts or tribunals. When an award is received by the concerned Assistant Labour Commissioner/Regional Labour Commissioner, (s)he tries to ascertain whether the award was implemented by the parties or not implemented or has it been modified or rejected by the competent government in its proceedings under Section 17A. In case of non-implementation, the Assistant Labour Commissioner/Regional Labour Commissioner can issue a show cause notice to the party at fault requesting information regarding why action should be taken against them. In case the defaulting party happens to be a public servant protected under Section 197 of the Criminal Procedure Code, prior permission of the government is needed before proceeding with prosecution. The power of judicial review of awards is limited to legality on grounds of jurisdictional defects, errors of law on the face of the record, or violation of the principles of natural justice. Section 17B of the Industrial Disputes Act affords a worker the right to receive the full wages last drawn during the pendency of the proceedings before a

High Court or the Supreme Court where the award of his/her reinstatement is challenged by the employer.

Unorganized Sector

Collective bargaining is rare in the unorganized sector. There are several instances of bipartite collective agreements in the unorganized sector that have provided for wages lower than the applicable minimum wages. Where such agreements are entered into through conciliation and/or registered with the appropriate government, the labour commissioners concerned are expected to ensure that the wages, benefits, and other terms and conditions are not less favourable than the applicable minimum wages and other standards laid down in labour laws.

Unfair Labour Practices

The Industrial Disputes Act, 1947 does not contain any stipulation that only a recognized union can raise an industrial dispute. In this, the Code of Discipline, 1958 is at variance with the Industrial Disputes Act. In 1982, the Industrial Disputes Act was amended to include the following as unfair labour practices: (*a*) refusal by the employer to bargain collectively in good faith with recognized trade unions; (*b*) refusal by a recognized union to bargain collectively in good faith with the employer; and (*c*) workers and trade unions of workers indulging in coercive activities against certification of a bargaining representative.

The collective bargaining rights of workers in the insurance sector, which has been a public sector monopoly, were curtailed by Parliament when it was found that collusive arrangements between unions and employers (public sector) were undermining the interests of policyholders. Now, insurance workers engage in consultations, but their pay revisions are notified unilaterally by the concerned government department. Of course, this curtailment does not apply to the private sector.

Section 2(p) of the Industrial Disputes Act, 1947 defines 'settlement' and Section 29 makes the breach of any term of the setdement punishable with imprisonment for a term of six months or with fine or both. Refusal to bargain collectively, in good faith, with recognized trade unions is an unfair labour practice under Section 2(ra)/Schedule V of the Act and is punishable under Section 25 (u) with imprisonment for a term which may extend to six months or with fine which may extend to ₹ 1,000 or both.

Several practices that qualify as unfair go unquestioned or unprosecuted. For instance, in one of the units of a multi-unit engineering company in north India, the management unilaterally declared a wage revision package after negotiations with the trade union broke down. The workers were 'happy' with the management's gesture; in fact, they left the next revision to the management's discretion as well. In another case, a multinational corporation near Delhi lured its workers with higher wages in return for not joining the trade union. Even in the public sector there have been occasions when supervisors have got benefits like interim relief pending wage revision only when they have given in writing that they will not join the union.

To the extent that managements are willing to pay a price to keep unions out, workers in India themselves contribute to making trade unions redundant in collective bargaining. Further, private sector companies, particularly pharmaceutical ones, often have designated sales representatives as officers and offer them additional benefits. Since this curtails job security, when sales representatives have protested and moved to court, the latter has held that a mere change in designation does not take away their right to unionize or disentitle them to job security.

LEVELS OF BARGAINING AND AGREEMENTS

In the following section, we shall discuss the various levels, duration, and coverage of agreements and international collective bargaining.

National-Level Agreements

Prior to the 1970s wage boards appointed by the government were giving awards on wages and working conditions. The number of wage boards declined from nineteen in the late 1960s to one (for journalists) in the late 1990s. Since the early 1970s sectoral bargaining at the national level is prevalent mainly in industries in which the government is the dominant player, for instance, banking and coal (approximately 700,000 workers each), steel and ports and docks (approximately 200,000 workers each). About sixty private, public and multinational banks are currently members of the Indian Banks' Association. They negotiate long-term settlements with the all-India federations of bank employees. In the coal sector, over 200 coking and non-coking mines across the country were nationalized in the early 1970s. However, since then to date there has been only one national agreement for the entire coal industry. In steel, there is a permanent bipartite committee for integrated steel mills in the public and private sectors. Since 1969, this committee, the National Joint Consultative Committee for Steel Industry (NJCS), has signed six long-term settlements. In the port sector, thirteen major ports have formed the Indian Ports' Association. They negotiate with the industrial federations of the major national trade union centres in the country.

A peculiar feature of national-level sectoral bargaining is the presence of a single employer body and the involvement of the concerned administrative ministry from the employers' side. In many sectors, negotiations are conducted by two to five major national trade union centres with a significant presence through their respective industry federations of workers' organizations. In banks, coal and ports and docks, all agreements have invariably been preceded by strikes or strike threats. It is only in the steel industry that this has not happened during the past three decades. Despite nationalization in the late 1970s, there is no industry-wide bargaining in the oil sector. The Oil Coordination Committees has, however, managed to achieve an appreciable level of standardization in pay and service conditions, even though collective bargaining takes place at die firm and/or plant level (for instance, Hindustan Petroleum Corporation Limited).

In India, civil servants' pay provides the base-mark for the public sector. In the public sector, competitive bargaining bases itself on the best bargain, invoking Article 12 of the Constitution of India which has in certain cases been interpreted by the Supreme Court to mean that the public sector is the State and hence cannot discriminate among its employees. Public sector pay in turn, provides the base-mark for unionized workers in the private sector, where collective bargaining has tended to become coercive, with employers often making the best of the current economic condition.

Industry-cum-region-wide Agreements

These are common across the private-sector-dominated cotton and jute, textile, engineering, and tea industries. However, such agreements are not binding on enterprise managements in the particular industry or region unless the managements authorize the respective worker organizations in writing to bargain on their behalf.

Firm/Plant-level Agreements

While employers generally prefer decentralized bargaining at the plant level, unions insist on bargaining at higher levels. They feel that plant-level bargaining reduces their bargaining power, particularly during periods of crisis. For instance, till 1990 in Escorts Limited, a private sector conglomerate with over fourteen factories and 35,000 workers, collective bargaining was used for the entire company. Post-liberalization when the management wanted to decentralize bargaining to die plant level, the union resisted and struck work for 39 days. This, however, did not deter the management from going ahead with decentralized bargaining based on die capacity to pay.

Duration of Agreements

Till the 1970s, the duration of collective agreements was usually two to diree years. During the 1970s and 1980s the duration increased to drree to four years. In the 1990s, over four-fifths of central public sector agreements were signed for five years each. Beginning from the sixth round of wage negotiations (1997 to date), the duration of wage agreements in the public sector has been raised from five to ten years. The validity of most of the collective agreements in the private sector, however, continues to be three or, in rare cases, four years. Some agreements, dealing exclusively with one aspect (such as incentives) have been for a period of six years.

Coverage

About 2% of the total workforce, or over 30% of the workers in the organized sector participate in collective bargaining. The legal framework encourages adjudication, with the government acting as the big brother. Most unions being highly politicized and the government wielding enormous discretionary power without the commensurate responsibility, legal administration becomes delinquent. Frequently, trade unions are co-opted into the collective bargaining process by either the government or the management. This leads to a crisis of confidence, particularly when unions find die going tough and are unable to meet the expectations of their members. As a resuit, workers' commitment to any solidarity-based ideology diminishes and they become increasingly instrumental in their orientation. They will not hesitate to shift their allegiance to another leader or union that promises more in less time, particularly, now that private sector managements want workers to do more for less. Labour is able to have its way in the product and labour market when conditions are not critical; but when they are, tiiere are tradeoffs: wage jobs, relay layoffs and take-money-and-leave (control over) jobs. If trade unions are still able to wield some influence, more so in the public sector, it is largely because coalition governments have been struggling for their own survival.

The disturbing reality is that workers can choose a union to represent them without belonging to it; workers can enjoy the benefits of collective bargaining as 'free riders' without joining a union or paying union dues; unions can have collective bargaining rights without workers' support; it is possible to strike deals with minority unions thus undermining the majority unions; and, workers' unity can be broken by offering more to the shrinking number of 'core' workers who do less and by paying less to the growing number of unorganized workers who do more.

International Collective Bargaining

In this era of globalization, global trade union federations and international trade union organizations have been striving hard to secure cross-border cooperation between trade unions and to coordinate worker representations and collective bargaining not only at local, industry and national level, but also at the regional (say, Europe-wide) and international level (covering whole sectors or several subsidiaries of a multinational). Though often workers have remained divided among themselves by economic self-interest within a country and thus, they find it hard to reach any common accord on specific strategies. Yet, the need for transnational worker solidarity is increasingly felt to meet the challenge of emerging employer strategies of global sourcing based on comparative cheap labour and cost cutting competitiveness.

International/global trade union federations are striving to establish minimum framework agreements that serve as benchmarks for their affiliate unions and sector-based federations (to begin within a region, say European Union) on collective bargaining. While employers want to compete on the basis of cheap labour, trade unions aim to take wages out of competition through coordinated international collective bargaining However, trade unions will find it hard to achieve their goals if they do not pay attention to the local concerns within and across countries. There is also the need to see how affiliate unions will continue to have national autonomy and yet coordinate their collective bargaining efforts at the regional/global level. The agenda includes not only a core demand on pay and working conditions but also a wide agenda including investment, training, employment creation, employability policies, and health and safety measures. The aim is to create a minimum set of labour standards applicable across the bargaining units. It is already beginning to happen through European Union-wide agreements. The consultative European works councils help provide the mechanism for the establishment of a transnational approach rooted in workplace realities. Since the adoption of the European Union directive on 22 September 1994, over 1000 workplaces have such workplace bodies. Over 100 firms have established global works councils. They have the potential to develop new forms of employee interest representation at transnational level, including the conclusion of framework agreements over aspects of employment and social policy and enhancing employee influence over management decisions in multinational corporations.

The 20-million-strong International Federation of Chemical, Energy, Mine and General Workers Union (ICEM), which was formed in January 1996 as a result of the merger of existing trade union organizations in the mining, chemical and sectors seeks to engage the multinationals in negotiated exchanges with trade unions at the global level. Such networks would not engage in international collective bargaining over wages, but provide a way of enforcing minimum codes of behaviour and agreed international standards at the company level worldwide in areas, such as skills training health, safety and environment. The 1994 agreement between the food, agriculture and allied workers' union International Union of Food Workers (IUF) and Danone. the France-based food conglomerate, is a good example. It commits both parties to monitor the observance of trade union rights in the company, negotiate and publicize collective bargaining agreements and ensure that union representatives have equal access to skill training and opportunities for promotion.

In 1998 ICEM brought unions from 10 countries together to launch a global strategy against the activities of Rio Tinto, the world's largest mining company. Particular attention was focused on die alleged anti-union policies of the firm, especially in its business operations in Australia, Portugal and Zimbabwe. In July 1998 ICEM signed the first ever industrial relations global agreement in the oil sector with Statoil, the Norwegian state oil company. This covered recognition of basic union rights, health, safety, environment, information, and training. It applies to all Statoil operations over which the company has a direct control. The agreement spells out explicitly its commitment to the ILO core labour standards. But in September Statoil found itself the focus of trade union attack for its links with the US anti-union compam Crown Central Petroleum which, refines its North Sea crude, oil for the American market.

The International Transport Workers' Federation (TIT) is developing a forward-looking strategy for transnational industrial relations. In July 1998 the ITF held'a meeting of affiliate unions in Miami covering the Americas where they tentatively agreed to develop closer cooperation, particularly within the emerging network of sub-regional free trade groupings led by NAFTA and MERCOSUR. It also formed a body to unite ITF affiliates within the European Union.

Trade unions are forming alliances with human rights groups to pressurize transnational companies to adopt codes of conduct for their foreign subsidiaries or suppliers. The ICFTU has developed a campaign for corporate codes of conduct on international labour rights.

There are difficulties in achieving international coordination and international collective bargaining. For instance, the structures and the concepts of trade unionism vary from one country to another. In countries like China there is no concept of collective bargaining while the transition economies have only recently begun their tryst with collective bargaining. Workers' economic interests also differ, with concerns about job shifts from developed to developing countries and later within developing countries themselves as employers pursue strategies to produce where it is cheapest and sell where their products can fetch the best price.

In multinational companies, trade unions at the international level have been pressing for world-wide works councils, regional or international framework agreements for different sectors and corporate codes through voluntary initiatives to avoid outsourcing to sweat shops. Difficulties persist here in enforcing labour codes of good behaviour in the contracting plants of several countries.

COLLECTIVE BARGAINING AND STAKEHOLDERS

Collective bargaining, as the term itself states, is a process that is not individualistic in nature, but collective. There are certain groups of stakeholders. During a negotiation the possible concerned parties are discussed below:

The Government

In western democracies, collective bargaining takes place in its most advanced form whereas, in communist countries, collective bargaining is not allowed. In transition economies like the former USSR (the CIS countries) and eastern and central Europe, collective bargaining agreements are beginning to take place. In centrally planned economies there is a fear that if collective bargaining is left to the parties, it will cause distortions in wage levels and unit labour costs. Therefore, it would be a tendency of the government to regulate wage increases. But wage controls would work for a short term, not over a period, particularly if such controls fail to pay attention to two other related areas: incomes and prices.

Democratic governments believe collective bargaining is a public policy aimed at promoting harmonious and cooperative relationships and encouraging the growth of strong and independent organizations of workers and employers. In some countries public policies dissuade parties from entering into collective bargaining agreements on issues other dian wages and working conditions.

One of the major concerns of governments, in countries that are wedded to the principles of egalitarianism, concerns the disparity and inequity that can occur between and across different sectors and the exploitation during conditions of tight labour markets (scarcity of labour with relevant skills) and by employers under adverse economic conditions.

The Employers/Management

The perspectives of management and workers or employers and unions are usually divergent and conflicting in a collective bargaining situation. If they are in an adversarial mode, their energies and efforts will be directed at barring the gain to the other party. If they realize the value of cooperation and collaboration, they would like to consult and cooperate to produce a bigger size cake and agree on each having a bigger slice than before.

Employers would find it easy to afford pay increases if the cost of such pay revision is funded through improvements in productivity and profitability. In the past managements used to receive charters of demands and bargain with unions and offer something. In return, management usually did not ask and therefore, did not get anything. Nevertheless, in the last one decade or so, managements have increasingly been making counter proposals and insisting on the policy of 'something for something nothing for nothing'. Thus collective bargaining has now truly become a give and take process.

For employers the advantage with collective bargaining is that they can secure some equity, fairness, and parity between and among workers. However, where managements bargain separately with different craft unions within an enterprise, it results in undesirable competition, disparity) and conflict.

The Workers/Trade Unions

It is generally recognized that under present day economic conditions an individual worker who is not in the organized sector and who is not unionized is generally unable to exercise much bargaining. The exception is the high-tech service sector where the tendency is generally not to join a union and to negotiate pay and benefits individually. Yet, for a large proportion of workforce in wage/salaried employment, collective bargaining is still supposed to increase the power of the workers and trade unions to negotiate better wages and conditions of employment. However, as we saw in an earlier chapter, the bargaining power of unions is high if both the input and output of labour is not substitutable and if the proportionate cost of labour is low. The purpose of trade unions is to secure more wages and benefits for their members and to ensure a semblance of parity across different categories of employees. The higher the level of coordination and centralization in bargaining the greater the tendency to show some moderation in wages so that the weak and strong units pay more or less similar wages to workers at similar skill levels and occupations. However, the current trends towards decentralization and individualization of contracts are negatively impinging on the power and outcomes of negotiations based on equity/parity.

The Consumers and Community

Where unions and managements enter into collusive agreements, they may prove detrimental to the interests of the consumers and community. In the late 1970s an agreement between the employees' union and the Life Insurance Corporation provided for granting additional benefits to employees financed from the profits that should have been passed on, at least partially, to policyholders because the profits accrued largely due to increased life expectancy. The result was that, in 1981, the Government introduced an amendment prohibiting them from entering into collective agreements in future. The ban continues to this day. In the 1980s, following Drug Price Controller Order, when the prices of some drugs were frozen or reduced, some pharma companies began to incur loss. They curtailed production within the company and began to outsource production to small-scale enterprises whereby they could get some concessions and reduce input costs, including wages. The resultant prohibits were shared by the company, its workers (who could not only save their jobs despite reduced production but also gained a bonanza for agreeing to transfer production to a third party), and the contract manufacturers. The workers who were engaged in the production of drugs in small-scale enterprises, however, got much lower wages than those in the big domestic and foreign companies.

Relations within the Enterprise

When the intention of the parties to a negotiation is to bar the other party from gaining, the relations tend to be adversarial. Even otherwise, collective bargaining, by nature is perceived to be oriented by conflicts of interests. The impact of collective bargaining on manager-employee relations is difficult to generalize. Generally speaking, collective bargaining does not address many manager-employee problems. Some managers may feel that they are placed in the conflicting, role of representing then-employees to management. It is not unusual to find some managers being drawn into petty, distracting, and time-consuming disputes. Where collective agreements restrain managers from directly communicating with employees, there are bound to be problems in communication.

Organizational Impact

Negotiations take place under conditions of unbalanced power relationships. There the impact of collective agreements on organizations, companies, and/or unions would be varied. When negotiations are deadlocked or take place under the influence and pressure tactics of outsiders, including the government, law and order enforcing machinery, and the public (in the case of public utilities), the locus of control shifts away from the enterprise and the outcomes become unpredictable for both the unions and managements. Therefore, it is in the interests of the parties to ensure that conflict does not escalate. Failure to negotiate may sometimes escalate the dispute into legal action.

NEGOTIATING TECHNIQUES AND SKILLS (C.B.)

Negotiation is a process in which two or more parties who have common and conflicting interests come together and talk with a view to reaching an agreement. Negotiation is concerned with purposeful persuasion and constructive compromise. It involves five key activities:

1. Obtaining *substantial results,* diving the co.st and benefits, and achieving the go dictated by the interests of both the company and the members of the true union.

2. Influencing the *balance of power* between parties. Balancing the company and the workers/members or making it a little more favourable to be workers/members.
3. Influencing the *atmosphere.* Promoting a constructive climate and positive personal relations between the trade union and members on the one hand and between the trade union and the management on the other.
4. Influencing the *constituency.* Reinforcing the position of trade union leadership with respect to the members on whose behalf the trade union leaders negotiate.
5. Influencing the *procedures.* Developing procedures that allow people to be while increasing the chances of reaching a favourable compromise. This is when one is able to distinguish between the interests of trade union members and taking positions on their behalf. Interests can be safeguarded in more than one way. If one takes a position, one limits the options.
   - Processes rather than outcomes are important to maintain long-term relationships. Temporary gains would be short-lived. But if the processes are appropriate, the trust and understanding generated will prove useful to all concerned over a period of time.
   - Results, not activities are important.
   - Give and take is important, not .giving in or surprising.

A negotiation could result in any one of the following situations:

- **Win-lose:** Herein, the negotiating parties think that 'winning is everything' or 'winning is the only thing'.
- **Lose-win:** One part}' achieves most and the other party loses or gains very little Here either party may consider that the 'relationship is paramount'.
- **Lose-Lose:** Both parties lose or do not get what they want and reflect an attitude of 'take it or leave it' or 'nothing for nothing'.

- **Win-Win:** Both parties get what they want. Instead of adopting an attitude of 'winning is everything' or 'winning is the only thing', the parties believe in mutual, gain.

Achieving win-win agreements requires integrating the interests of both/all the parties. This means that the parties should keep the following points in mind while negotiating.

1. *Focus on their interests, not take positions:* For an employer to say, 'I cannot pay you more' is taking a position. If the employer says, 'I can pay you more if the unit labour cost remains the same' it means safeguarding one's interest.
2. *Focus on the problem, not the person:* It is easy to take things personally even in the professional world, but that is a state of mind that needs to be eliminated, especially during negotiations. Getting; personal or disparaging only shows a lack of respect and trust, which can result in the failure of the negotiation process. For example, let us consider the oid cats-and-monkey story. Two cats are quarrelling over sharing a load of bread. Neither would trust the other. They trusted the monkey and lost the whole bread. If they focused on the problem, they could have agreed that one would cut into two halves arid the other would choose. The question of trust or the lack of trust would not have come, in the way of solving the problem.
3. *Invent multiple solutions:* If the parties in a negotiation think selfishly, the negotiation process can fail. Instead, it is essential that all the interests of all the parties are discussed and solutions are sought that lead to the satisfaction of either all or a majority of the parties. The following example will help in driving the point home. Two young daughters were quarrelling over the only orange left in the house. Both wanted the whole orange. The mother spoke to both of them separately. The elder one wanted the peel for making the Christmas pudding.

The younger one wanted to eat the orange. The mother skilfully peeled the orange and gave the orange peel to the elder daughter and the fruit to the younger one. Both were happy.

4. *Be creative:* Sometimes problematic situations seem too far advanced to be helped by negotiations. When things are tough, it is time to employ some creativity. Creative handling of negotiations and creative solutions can make sure that all the parties are happy with the outcome(s). In the King Solomon story, when two mothers were claiming the motherhood of a young boy, the king asked the butcher to cut the child into two halves and distribute among the two ladies. The real mother panicked and asked the king to give the child to the other lady so that her child may live. Thus, the king was able to find the real mother.
5. *Expand the pie:* Employers should think of paying more wages to their employees without increasing costs. Savings need not come from labour, but the creative use of labour does reduce non-labour costs. In most cases, labour costs are less than 15% of the total ex-factory costs and 5% or so of the final price that the consumer pays.
6. *Non-specific compensation:* Give the other parties something that is valued more by them but not much by you.
7. *Log rolling:* Where the agenda or the charter of demands and counter demands is long and complex with differing priorities, go over the list and begin with those points which the parties have a common interest to resolve. Building on the understanding gained in the process, it is possible to move forward towards art amicable solution.
8. *Bridge the gap in perceptions through reformulation of the issue:* Usually, how an issue is framed makes a difference to the negotiation. Look at both the giving end and the

receiving end rather than taking one side. Consider the consequences of agreeing or not agreeing to a proposal. In case of technological changes, one must look at both the consequences of change and the consequences of no change.

Stages of Negotiation

There are four stages of negotiation—preparation, discussion, bargaining and agreement.

Preparation

To fail to prepare is to prepare to fail. Preparations entail the following:

(*i*) *Collecting information:* Facts on relevant aspects are needed to produce enough evidence to substantiate one's demands/arguments.

(*ii*) *Setting objectives:* Ideal, targeted, and resistance positions should be decided upon. For instance, 15% wage rise is ideal, 12% target, but wage rise below the rate of inflation is the resistance point because it will mean erosion of real earnings.

(*iii*) *Establishing priorities:* Distinguish between what must be achieved and what might be achieved.

(*iv*) *Assessing the other party and its case:* To counter the other party's arguments, it is necessary to study its needs, strengths, and compulsions well enough in advance.

(*v*) *Noting details:* Take precise notes of who said what at every stage of the negotiation process. Leave space for details and to record your arguments.

Bargaining

Negotiations should yield something for all the concerned parties. While bargaining, it would be best to keep the following points in mind:

(*i*) There cannot be any bargaining if either party takes a fixed stand and is unwilling to move from a set position, (*ii*) Parties should be willing to make compromises, offer concessions and develop packages that are mutually beneficial.

(*iii*) If there is a stalemate or deadlock in negotiations because either party does not agree to what the other says or resorts to threats and bluffs—consider different ways of dealing with these situations.

(*iv*) Try to understand the issues rather than be emotional about them or take things personally.

(*v*) Focus on the problem and interests rather than focusing on the person(s) and taking positions.

Factors Contributing to the Success or Failure of Collective Bargaining

1. *Knowledge, awareness and skill as ingredients for participation in the process of collective bargaining:* Workers are generally lacking awareness and skills, as are their representatives from trade unions. This is an important part of workers' education which is overlooked today and both in content and process, results in unprepared the workers. Knowledge, awareness and skills are relevant for manufacturing concerns, valid in the following areas:
    - Installed capacity
    - Production capacity
    - Percentage of production capacity in relation to installed capacity
    - The causes and contributory factors for a heavy gap
    - Raw material, source of procurement, quality, transportation, grading, etc.
    - Knowledge of 'product mix'.
    - Element of wastage and leakage of raw materials.
    - Manpower planning, nuances of industrial engineering (job steady, classification, description/

analysis), concept of 'right man for right job', job training (extent, adequacy and effectiveness).

- Planning for inventory control
- Concept of a captive suit, concept of ancillary linkage between a mother plant and its units

2. *Centralization vs. decentralization and delegation:* Collective bargaining fails when power is centralized in the board at plant level; and when the representative of the management, sitting at one end of the table, cannot take decisions because s/he has no delegated power and it takes time to seek out the powers and obtain something from them.
3. *The use of language, patience, civility, courtesy, and decorum:* It can be said that good language unites, whereas bad language alienates. As such, good language, courtesy, and decorum are part of the manners under parental purview, but they can also be the outcome of exposure to life and training.
4. *Backseat pedaling/driving:* Talks fail due to extraneous factors/influences and not so much because of the merit or demerit of the talk theme. Backseat driving is the result of political considerations (a superior and influential force dictating their vested interests to whomever they lend support) and could be totally demoralizing/demotivating for the parties to the dispute, as well as the conciliation machinery.
5. *Openness and transparency in information sharing are the worst casualties:* Collective bargaining can be a credible and sustainable exercise only if there is complete honesty and transparency; talks should not be shrouded in secrecy or games of hide and seek. In actual practice, collective bargaining becomes a game of dice where the other party's next move is anybody's guess. Access to information is halted by varied hindrances that heighten feelings of, distrust and suspicion, with the inevitable conseqnences.

Closure and Agreement

Keep the following in mind while concluding an agreement:

(*i*) Define the scope of the agreement, that is, to whom it applies,

(*ii*) Define the time-frame/duration of the agreement,

(*iii*) Write down clearly what has been agreed,

(*iv*) Specify the conditions, if any, for making the agreement operational and the consequences of non-compliance to obligations of both the parties as a result of the agreement,

(*v*) Lay down the procedure for dealing with problems of interpretation and implementation,

(*vi*) Take your party members into confidence and brief them about the content of the agreement before it is formalized,

(*vii*) Sign the agreement. If the legal framework warrants, get the agreement registered with the competent authority in the government,

(*viii*) Circulate copies of the agreement among the members.

(*ix*) Be tactful while going to the media and issuing statements:

- Do not escalate expectations or tensions.
- Do not allow yourself to lose face.
- Do not cause loss of face to the other party.
- Let the other stakeholders (consumers, community, etc.) not get the feeling that your party is gaining at their expense.

Conditions for Mutual Gains Bargaining

There are certain conditions which facilitate the process of collective bargaining. Some of these are as follows:

- a favourable political climate and an institutional framework that encourages collective bargaining
- recognition of the right of (*a*) freedom of association and (*b*) collective bargaining
- strong and well-developed unions of workers and employers

- recognition of unions and their role at micro and macro levels
- goodwill on both sides
- mutual exchange of information
- willingness to find common interests
- realization of interdependence between and among the parties concerned
- a balance of power between the parties because negotiations between parties with power differences cannot produce fair agreements
- acting in good faith
- mutual respect
- a desire for mutual gain

SECTION-C

CHAPTER

5 Indian Labour Market

Introduction

Usually an informal market where workers find paying work, employers find willing workers and were wage rates are determined. Labor markets may be local or national (even international) in their scope and are made up of smaller, interacting labor markets for different qualifications, skills and geographical locations. They depend on exchange of information between employers and job seekers about wage rates, conditions of employment, level of competition and job location.

Flexibility of Indian Labour Market

India is a very young country. The data on demographics suggest that majority of the Indian population is under the age of 25. Also, about 140 million people will be joining the workforce in the next decade. The numbers sound very encouraging, painting the picture of an economy where growth is going to be the norm for the coming years.

While the most important issue taken with this consideration, is obviously job growth. Much hyped is the growth in IT and BPO sectors across televisions and magazines, which in absolute terms is going to be only 1 million or maybe 2 million. With the current labour force of 400 million only 7% are employed in the formal sector. Characteristic of the Indian labour market is the informal sector that makes up for the rest 93% of the job opportunities.

The discrepancy in the estimated growth of labour force and the growth of jobs is evident. It is an issue that has been talked about at various levels, resulting in numerous methods that could check it. Lesser popularized and equally important are the issues of labour market flexibility, that have a similar bearing on the equity and efficiency of an economy.

Robert M Solow identified the attributes of an inflexible labour market to be as follows: "A labour market is inflexible if the level of unemployment - insurance benefits is too high or their duration is too long, or if there are many restrictions on the freedom of employers to fire and to hire, or if the permissible hours of work are too tightly regulated, or if excessive generous compensation for overtime work is mandated, or if trade unions have too much power to protect incumbent workers against competition and to control the follow of work at the site of production, or perhaps if statutory health and safety regulations are too stringent."

In India, labour unions and laws that bind the labour movement create such inflexibility. The unions manage to set the wage above the market rate of wage, which in turn reduce the capacity of firm to hire workers, causing unemployment. The increased cost of production also crowds out investment, resulting in welfare loss. In trying to protect the interest of workers in the firm, such rigidity set by the union affects interest of those who are unemployed.

As is apparent, post globalization, the capital movement has been more flexible than labour. The labour flow is restricted not just between countries, but within the same country as well. Flexibility in this market can be achieved by removal or reduction of legislation that protects the labour market. The million-dollar question is—Will such flexibility be desirable? Liberal economists would argue that such a free movement of labour would ensure competitive market equilibrium. The free market for labour will entail better efficiency and productivity. State intervention will create distortions in the market and will deviate the equilibrium from the best possible outcome.

Critics of de-regulation argue that if the firms in a free labour market compete on the basis of lower wage, then there is no incentive for them to work on innovation of technology or increasing productivity. Only when the path to competition on the basis of low wages and bad working conditions is barred by providing a floor of labour standards, the firms can become enterprising and invest in technological and organizational innovation, which, in turn, leads to better wages and working conditions. Also, an absence of rules and regulations, when hiring workers may lead to deplorable working conditions for the workers.

The current policy on labour flexibility needs a redesign as it has invited criticism from the employer and the workers. Since labour cannot be treated like a commodity that is exchanged for production, with tribulations like job security, minimum wage, social security, trade union right etc to be taken care of for purpose of development. Also too much restriction on its movement may cause unemployment. International experience suggests a middle path constructed keeping in view the dynamics of the domestic market, should be followed.

Principles of Wage Determination

As the major production cost, wages affect profits, business investment, competitiveness and are a cost push inflationary factor. As the major income in the economy, wages affect standard of living, income distribution and poverty and demand pull inflation.

At the source of wage disputes is the employer treating wages as their major cost and the employee viewing wages as their major income. The following principles have always been the bases of the wage determination process. All are economically valid. At different stages they have collectively, and singularly, been used to determine wage increases.

1. *Preserving real income:* This is the argument used by employees and Unions viewing wages as an income. Following this principle usually results in wages being indexed to inflation. In periods of rising inflation, indexation becomes a problem of an institutionalised wage-price spiral. Underlying aspects that have also impacted on real wage preservation arguments have been a "basic" minimum wage and comparative wage justice.

2. *Labour productivity:* A valid economic theory connects wages to labour productivity. Conflict arises over the measurement of productivity. Rewarding labour with a wage increase when technology and/or capital investment, increases labour efficiency, may not be justified.
3. *The capacity of business to afford wage increases:* This emphasises wages as a cost of production, and the threat of wage increases to squeeze profits. This "capacity" argument is that followed by business owners.
4. *The capacity of the economy to absorb wage increases:* This "capacity" argument views the macro impact of wage increases on inflation, competitiveness, and other aspects of internal and external balance; as well as the affect on business profits and investment from 3. This is the main argument of the Federal Government recognising the macro policy potential of an Incomes Policy to address external and internal balance goals to supplement demand management policies and the effects on income distribution.

The Methods of Wage Determination

Generally wage determination can be through a centralised, regulated, institutionalised system, or a decentralised system. Collective bargaining is when workers with similar employment conditions and skills unite, usually through a union, to present their wage demands to their employer(s). Enterprise bargaining is when workers at the same plant bargain with the employer. An award is an agreement that sets out both wages and working conditions. Our reliance on a centralised system, often based on indexation, has dominated wage determination over the last century.

The Payment of Wages Act, 1936

An Act to regulate the payment of wages to certain classes of 2 [employed persons].

Whereas it is expedient to regulate the payment of wages to certain classes of employed persons.

It is hereby enacted as follows:

Short Title, Extent, Commencement and Application

(1) This Act may be called the Payment of Wages Act, 1936.

(2) It extends to the whole of India.

(3) It shall come into force on such date as the Central Government may, by notification in the Official Gazette, appoint.

(4) It applies in the first instance to the payment of wages to persons employed in any factory, to persons] employed (otherwise than in a factory) upon any railway by a railway administration or, either directly or through a sub-contractor, by a person fulfilling a contract with a railway administration and to persons employed in an industrial or other establishment specified in sub-clauses (a) to (g) of clause (ii) of section 2.

(5) The State Government may, after giving three months' notice of its intention of so doing, by notification in the Official Gazette, extend the provisions of this Act or any of them to the payment of wages to any class of persons employed in any establishment or class of establishments specified by the Central Government or a State Government under sub-clause (h) of clause (ii) of section 2:

Provided that in relation to any such establishment owned by the Central Government, no such notification shall be issued except with the concurrence of that Government.

(6) Nothing in this Act shall apply to wages payable in respect of a wage-period which, over such wage-period, average one thousand six hundred rupees a month or more.

Definitions

In this Act, unless there is anything repugnant in the subject or context:

(*i*) "employed person" includes the legal representative of a deceased employed person;

(*ia*) "employer" includes the legal representative of a deceased employer;

(*ib*) "factory" means a factory as defined in clause (m) of section 2 of the Factories Act, 1948 (63 of 1948), and includes any place to which the provisions of that Act have been applied under subsection (1) of section 85 thereof;

(*ii*) "industrial or other establishment" means:

(*a*) tramway service, or motor transport service engaged in carrying passengers or goods or both by road for hire or reward;

(*aa*) air transport service other than such service belonging to, or exclusively employed in the military, or air forces of the Union or the Civil Aviation Department of the Government of India;

(*b*) dock, wharf or jetty;

(*c*) inland vessel, mechanically propelled;

(*d*) mine, quarry or oilfield;

(*e*) plantation;

(*f*) workshop or other establishment in which articles are produced, adapted or manufactured, with a view to their use, transport or sale;

(*g*) establishment in which any work relating to the construction, development or maintenance of buildings, roads, bridges or canals, or relating to operations connected with navigation, irrigation or the supply of water, or relating to the generation, and distribution of electricity or any other form of power is being carried on;

(*h*) any other establishment or class of establishments which the Central Government or a State Government may, having regard to the nature thereof, the need for protection of persons employed therein and other relevant circumstances, specify, by notification in the Official Gazette.

Wages

"Wages" means all remuneration (whether by way of salary, allowances or otherwise) expressed in terms of money or capable of being so expressed which would, if the terms of employment, express or implied, were fulfilled, be payable to a person employed in respect of his employment or of work done in such employment and includes:

(*a*) any remuneration payable under any award or settlement between the parties or order of a Court;

(*b*) any remuneration to which the person employed is entitled in respect of overtime work or holidays or any leave period;

(*c*) any additional remuneration payable under the terms of employment (whether called a bonus or by any other name);

(*d*) any sum which by reason of the termination of employment of the person employed is payable under any law, contract or instrument which provides for the payment of such sum, with or without deductions, but does not provide for the time within which the payment is to be made;

(*e*) any sum to which the person employed is entitled under any scheme framed under any law for the time being in force; but does not include:

(1) any bonus (whether under a scheme of profit sharing or otherwise) which does not form part of the remuneration payable under the terms of employment or which is not payable under any award or settlement between the parties or order of a Court;

(2) the value of any house-accommodation, or of the supply of light, water, medical attendance or

other amenity or of any service excluded from the computation of wages by a general or special order of the State Government;

(3) any contribution paid by the employer to any pension or provident fund and the interest which may have accrued thereon;

(4) any travelling allowance or the value of any travelling concession;

(5) any sum paid to the employed person to defray special expenses entailed on him by the nature of his employment; or

(6) any gratuity payable on the termination of employment in cases other than those specified in sub-clause (d).

Responsibility for Payment of Wages

Every employer shall be responsible for the payment to persons employed by him of all wages required to be paid under this Act: Provided that, in the case of persons employed (otherwise than by a contractor):

(*a*) in factories, if a person has been named as the manager of the factory under [clause (f) of sub-section (1) of section 7 of the Factories Act, 1948 (63 of 1948),

2*[(*b*) in industrial or other establishments, if there is a person responsible to the employer for the supervision and control of the industrial or other establishments;

(*c*) upon railways (otherwise than in factories), if the employer is the railway administration and the railway administration has nominated a person in this behalf for the local area concerned; the person so named, the person so responsible to the employer, or the person so nominated, as the case may be, [shall also be responsible lor such payment.

Fixation of Wage-periods

1. Every person responsible for the payment of wages under section 3 shall fix periods (in this Act referred to

as wage-periods) in respect of which such wages shall be payable.

2. No wage-period shall exceed one month.

Time of Payment of Wages

1. The wages of every person employed upon or in—
   (*a*) any railway, factory or industrial or other establishment upon or in which less than one thousand persons are employed, shall be paid before the expiry of the seventh day,
   (*b*) any other railway, factory or industrial or other establishment], shall be paid before the expiry of the tenth day, after the last day of the wage-period in respect of which the wages are payable:

   Provided that in the case of persons employed on a dock, wharf or jetty or in a mine, the balance of wages found due on completion of the final tonnage account of the ship or wagons loaded or unloaded, as the case may be, shall be paid before the expiry of the seventh day from the day of such completion.
2. Where the employment of any person is terminated by or on behalf of the employer, the wages earned by him shall be paid before the expiry of the second working day from the day on which his employment is terminated:

   Provided that where the employment of any person in an establishment is terminated due to the closure of the establishment for any reason other than a weekly or other recognised holiday, the wages earned by him shall be paid before the expiry of the second day from the day on which his employment is so terminated.
3. The State Government may, by general or special order, exempt, to such extent and subject to such conditions as may be specified in the order, the person responsible for the payment of wages to persons employed upon any railway (otherwise than in a factory) or to persons employed as daily-rated workers in the Public Works Department of the Central Government or the State

Government] from the operation of this section in respect of the wages of any such persons or class of such persons:

Provided that in the case of persons employed as daily-rated workers as aforesaid, no such order shall be made except in consultation with the Central Government.

(4) Save as otherwise provided in sub-section (2), all payments] of wages shall be made on a working day.

Wages to be Paid in Current Coin or Currency Notes

All wages shall be paid in current coin or currency notes or in both:

Provided that the employer may, after obtaining the written authorisation of the employed person, pay him the wages either by cheque or by crediting the wages in his bank account.

Deductions which may be Made from Wages

1. Notwithstanding the provisions of sub-section (2) of section 47 of the Indian Railways Act, 1890 (9 of 1890), the wages of an employed person shall be paid to him without deductions of any kind except those authorised by or under this Act. 1

   Explanation I— Every payment made by the employed person to the employer or his agent shall, for the purposes of this Act, be deemed to be a deduction from wages.

   Explanation II—Any loss of wages resulting from the imposition, for good and sufficient cause, upon a person employed of any of the following penalties, namely

   (*i*) the withholding of increment or promotion (including the stoppage of increment at an efficiency bar);

   (*ii*) the reduction to a lower post or time scale or to a lower stage in a time scale; or

   (*iii*) suspension; shall not be deemed to be a deduction from wages in any case where the rules framed by the employer for the imposition of any such penalty are in conformity with the requirements, if any, which may be specified in this behalf by the State Government by notification in the Official Gazette.

2. Deductions from the wages of an employed person shall be made only in accordance with the provisions of this Act, and may be of the following kinds only, namely -
   (*a*) fines;
   (*b*) deductions for absence from duty;
   (*c*) deductions for damage to or loss of goods expressly entrusted to the employed person for custody, or for loss of money for which he is required to account, such damage or loss is directly attributable to his neglect or default;
   3(*d*) deductions for house-accommodation supplied by the employer or by Government or any housing board set up under any law for the time being in force (whether the Government or the board is the employer or not) or any other authority engaged in the business of subsidising house-accommodation which may be specified in this behalf by the State Government by notification in the Official Gazette;
   (*e*) deductions for such amenities and services supplied by the employer as the State Government or any officer specified by it in this behalf may, by general or special order, authorise. Explanation.—The word "services" in this clause does not include the supply of tools and raw materials required for the purposes of employment;
   (*f*) deductions for recovery of advances of whatever nature (including advances for travelling allowance or conveyance allowance) and the interest due in respect thereof, or for adjustment of over-payments of wages;
   (*ff*) deductions for recovery of loans made from any fund for the welfare of labour in accordance with the rules approved by the State Government, and the interest due in respect thereof;
   (*fff*) deductions for recovery of loans granted for house-building or other purposes approved by the

State Government and the interest due in respect thereof;

(*g*) deductions of income-tax payable by the employed person;

(*h*) deductions required to be made by order of a Court or other authority competent to make such order;

(*i*) deductions for subscriptions to, and for repayment of advances from any provident fund to which the Provident Funds Act, 1925 (19 of 1925), applies or any recognised provident fund as defined in section 58A of the Indian Income-tax Act, 1922 (11 of 1922), or any provident fund approved in this behalf by the State Government, during the continuance of such approval;

(*j*) deductions for payments to co-operative societies approved by the State Government or any officer specified by it in this behalf] or to a scheme of insurance maintained by the Indian Post Office; 6

(*k*) deductions, made with the written authorisation of the person employed for payment of any premium on his life insurance policy to the Life Insurance Corporation of India established under the Life Insurance Corporation Act, 1956 (31 of 1956), or for the purchase of securities of the Government of India or of any State Government or for being deposited in any Post Office Savings Bank in furtherance of any savings scheme of any such Government.

[(*kk*) deductions made, with the written authorisation of the person, for the payment of his contribution to any fund by the employer or a trade union registered under the Trade Unions Act, 1926 for the welfare of the employed persons or the members of their families, or both and approved by the State Government or any officer specified by it in this behalf, during the continuance of such approval;

(*kkk*) deductions made, with the written authorisation of the employed person, for payment of the fees payable by him for the membership of any trade union registered under the Trade Unions Act, 1926;

(*l*) deductions for payment of insurance premia on Fidelity Guarantee Bonds;

(*m*) deductions for recovery of losses sustained by a railway administration on account of acceptance by the employed person of counterfeit or base coins or mutilated or forged currency notes;

(*n*) deductions for recovery of losses sustained by a railway administration on account of the failure of the employed person to invoice, to bill, to collect or to account for the appropriate charges due to that administration; whether in respect of fares, freight, demurrage, wharfage and cranage or in respect of sale of food in catering establishments or in respect of sale of commodities in grain shops or otherwise;

(*o*) Deductions for recovery of losses sustained by a railway administration on account of any rebates or refunds incorrectly granted by the employed person where such loss is directly attributable to his neglect or default;

(*p*) deductions, made with the written authorisation of the employed person, for contribution to the Prime Minister's National Relief Fund or to such other Fund as the Central Government may, by notification in the Official Gazette, specify;

(*q*) deductions for contributions to any insurance scheme framed by the Central Government for the benefit of its employees.

Notwithstanding anything contained in this Act, the total amount of deductions which may be made under sub-section (2) in any wage period from the wages of any employed person shall not exceed—

(*i*) in cases where such deductions are wholly or partly made for payments to cooperative societies under clause (*j*) sub-section (2), seventy-five per cent of such wages, and

(*ii*) in any other case, fifty per cent, of such wages: Provided that where the total deductions authorised under sub-section (2) exceed seventy-five per cent, or, as the case may be, fifty per cent, of the wages, the excess may be recovered in such manner as may be prescribed.

Nothing contained in this section shall be construed as precluding the employer from recovering from the wages of the employed person or otherwise any amount payable by such person under any law for the time being in force other than the Indian Railways Act, 1890 (9 of 1890).

Fines

1. No fine shall be imposed on any employed person save in respect of such acts and omissions on his part as the employer, with the previous approval of the State Government or of the prescribed authority, may have specified by notice under sub-section (2).
2. A notice specifying such acts and omissions shall be exhibited in the prescribed manner on the premises in which the employment is carried on or in the case of person employed upon a railway (otherwise than in a factory), at the prescribed place or places.
3. No fine shall be imposed on any employed person until he has been given ah opportunity of showing cause against the fine, or otherwise than in accordance with such procedure as may be prescribed for the imposition of fines.
4. The total amount of fine which may be imposed in any one wage-period on any employed person shall not exceed an amount equal to three per cent. of the wages payable to him in respect of that wage-period.

5. No fine shall be imposed on any employed person who is under the age of fifteen years.
6. No fine imposed on any employed person shall be recovered from him by instalments or after the expiry of sixty days from the day on which it was imposed.
7. Every fine shall be deemed to have been imposed on the day of the act or omission in respect of which it was imposed.

All fines and ail realisations thereof shall be recorded in a register to be kept by the person responsible for the payment of wages under section 3 in such form as may be prescribed; and all such realisations shall be applied only to such purposes beneficial to the persons employed in the factory or establishment as are approved by the prescribed authority. Explanation. When the persons employed upon or in any railway, factory or l*[industrial or other establishement] are part only of a staff employed under the same management, all such realisations may be credited to a common fund maintained for the staff as a whole, provided that the fund shall be applied only to such purposes as are approved by the prescribed authority.

Deductions for Absence from Duty

1. Deductions may be made under clause (b) of sub-section (2) of section 7 only on account of the absence of an employed person from the place or places where, by the terms of his employment, he is required to work, such absence being for the whole or any part of the period during which he is so required to work.
2. The amount of such deduction shall in no case bear to the wages payable to the employed person in respect of the wage-period for which the deduction is made a larger proportion than the period for which he was absent bears to the total period, within such wage-period, during which by the terms of his employment, he was required to work: Provided that, subject to any rules made in this behalf by the State Government, if ten or more employed persons acting in concert absent themselves without due

notice (that is to say without giving the notice which is required under the terms of their contracts of employment) and without reasonable cause, such deduction from any such person may include such amount not exceeding his wages for eight days as may be any such terms be due to the employer in lieu of due notice.

Explanation—For the purposes of this section, an employed person shall be deemed to be absent from the place where he is required to work if, although present in such place, he refuses, in pursuance of a stay-in strike or for any other cause which is not reasonable in the circumstances, to carry out his work.

Deductions for Damage or Loss

(1) deduction under clause (c) or clause (o) of sub-section (2) of section 7 shall not exceed the amount of the damage or loss caused to the employer by the neglect or default of the employed person.

(1A) A deduction shall not be made under clause (c) or clause (m) or clause (n) or clause (o) of subsection (2) of section 7 until the employed person has been given an opportunity of showing cause against the deduction, or otherwise than in accordance with such procedure as may be prescribed for the making of such deductions.]

(2) All such deductions and all realisations thereof shall be recorded in a register to be kept by the person responsible for the payment of wages under section 3 in such form as may be prescribed.

Deductions for Services Rendered

A deduction under clause (d) or clause (e) of sub-section (2) of section 7 shall not be made from the wages of an employed person, unless the house-accommodation amenity or service has been accepted by him, as a term of employment or otherwise, and such deduction shall not exceed an amount equivalent to the value of the house-accommodation amenity or service supplied and in the case of a deduction under the said clause (e), shall be subject to such conditions as the State Government may impose.

12- Deductions under clause (0 of sub-section (2) of section 7 shall be subject to the following conditions, namely—

(*a*) recovery of an advance of money given before employment began shall be made from the first payment of wages in respect of a complete wage-period, but no recovery shall be made of such advances given for travelling-expenses;

(*aa*) recovery of an advance of money given after employment began shall be subject to such conditions as the State Government may impose;]

(*b*) recovery of advances of wages not already earned shall be subject to any rules made by the State Government regulating the extent to which such advances may be given and the instalments by which they may be recovered.

Deductions for Recovery of Loans

shall be subject to any rules made by the State Government regulating the extent to which such loans may be granted and the rate of interest payable thereon.

Deductions for payments to co-operative societies and insurance schemes.

Deductions under clause (j) and clause (k) of sub-section (2) of section 7 shall be subject to such conditions as the State Government may impose.

Maintenance of Registers and Records

1. Every employer shall maintain such registers and records giving such particulars of persons employed by him, the work performed by them, the wages paid to them, the deductions made from their wages, the receipts given by them and such other particulars and in such form as may be prescribed.
2. Every register and record required to be maintained under this section shall, for the purposes of this Act, be

preserved for a period of three years after the date of the last entry made therein.

Inspectors

1. An Inspector of Factories appointed under sub-section (1) of section 8 of the Factories Act, 1948 (63 of 1948), shall be an Inspector for the purposes of this Act in respect of all factories within the local limits assigned to him.

2. The State Government may appoint Inspectors for the purposes of this Act in respect of all *persons employed upon 3 railway (otherwise than in a factory) to whom this Act applies.*

3. The State Government may, by notification in the Official Gazette, appoint such other persons as it thinks fit to be Inspectors for the purposes of this Act and may define the local limits within which and the class of factories and industrial or other establishments in respect of which they shall exercise their functions.

4. Inspector may:

(*a*) make such examination and inquiry as he thinks fit in order to ascertain whether the provisions of this Act or rules made there under are being observed;

(*b*) with such assistance, if any, as he thinks fit, enter, inspect and search any premises of any railway, factory or industrial or other establishment at any reasonable time for the purpose of carrying out the objects of this Act;

(*c*) Supervise the payment of wages to persons employed upon any railway or in any factory or industrial or other establishment;

(*d*) Require by a written order the production at such place, as may be prescribed, of any register or record maintained in pursuance of this Act and take on the spot or otherwise statements of any persons which he may consider necessary for carrying out the purposes of this Act;

(*e*) seize or take copies of such registers or documents or portions thereof as he may consider relevant in respect of an offence under this Act which he has reason to believe has been committed by an employer;

(*f*) exercise such other powers as may be prescribed:

Provided that no person shall be compelled under this sub-section to answer any question or make any statement tending to incriminate himself.

(4A) The provisions of the code of Criminal Procedure, 1973 (2 of 1974) shall, so far as may be, apply to any search or seizure under this sub-section as the apply to any search or seizure made under the authority of a warrant issued under section 94] of the said Code.

(5) Every Inspector shall be deemed to be a public servant within the meaning of the Indian Penal Code (45 of 1860).

Facilities to be Afforded to Inspectors

Every employer shall afford an Inspector all reasonable facilities for making any entry, inspection, supervision, examination or inquiry under this Act.

Claims arising out of deductions from wages or delay in payment of wages and penalty for malicious or vexatious claims:

Provided that where the State Government considers it necessary so to do, it may appoint more than one authority for any specified area and may, by general or special order, provide for the distribution or allocation of work to be performed by them under this Act.

(2) Where contrary to the provisions of this Act any deduction has been made from the wages of an employed person, or any payment of wages has been delayed, such person himself, or any legal practitioner or any official of a registered trade union authorised in writing to act on his behalf, or any Inspector under this Act, or any other person acting with the permission of the authority appointed under sub-section (1), may apply to such authority for a direction under sub-section (3):

Provided further that any application may be admitted after the said period of twelve months when the applicant satisfies the authority that he had sufficient cause for not making the application within such period.

(3) When any application under sub-section (2) is entertained, the authority shall hear the applicant and the employer or other person responsible for the payment of wages under section 3, or give them an opportunity of being heard and after such further inquiry (if any) as may be necessary, may, without prejudice to any other penalty to which such employer or other person is liable under this Act, direct the refund to the employed person of the amount deducted, or the payment of the delayed wages, together with the payment of such compensation as the authority may think fit, not exceeding ten times the amount deducted in the former case and not exceeding twenty-five rupees in the latter, and even if the amount deducted or the delayed wages are paid before the disposal of the application, direct the payment of such compensation, as the authority may think fit, not exceeding twenty-five rupees:

Provided that no direction for the payment of compensation shall be made in the case of delayed wages if the authority is satisfied that the delay was due to:

(*a*) a bona fide error or bona fide dispute as to the amount payable to the employed person, or

(*b*) the occurrence of an emergency, or the existence of exceptional circumstances, such that the person responsible for the payment of the wages was unable, exercising reasonable diligence, to make prompt payment, or

(*c*) the failure of the employed person to apply for or accept payment.

If the authority hearing an application under this section is satisfied:

(*a*) that the application was either malicious or vexatious, authority may direct that a penalty not exceeding fifty rupees be paid to the employer or other person responsible for the payment of wages by the person presenting the application; or

(*b*) that in any case in which compensation is directed to be paid under sub-section (3), the applicant ought not to have been compelled to seek redress under this section, authority may direct that a penalty not exceeding fifty rupees be paid to the State Government by the employer or other person responsible for the payment of wages.

(4A) Where there is any dispute as to the person or persons being the legal representative or representatives of the employer or of the employed person, the decision of the authority on such dispute shall be final.

(4B) Any inquiry under this section shall be deemed to be a judicial proceeding within the meaning of sections 193, 219 and 228 of the Indian Penal Code (45 of I860).]

Any amount directed to be paid under this section may be recovered:

(*a*) if the authority is a Magistrate, by the authority as if it were a fine imposed by him as Magistrate, and

(*b*) if the authority is not a Magistrate, by any Magistrate to whom the authority makes application in this behalf, if it were a fine imposed by such Magistrate.

Single Application in Respect of Claims from Unpaid Group

(1) Employed persons are said to belong to the same unpaid group if they are borne on the same establishment and if l*[deductions have been made from their wages in contravention of this Act for the same cause and during the same wage-period or periods or if their wages for the same wage-period or periods have remained unpaid after the day fixed by section 5.

(2) A single application may be presented under section 15 on behalf or in respect of any number of employed persons belonging to the same unpaid group and in such case every person on whose behalf such application is presented may be awarded maximum compensation to the extent specified in sub-section (3) of section 15.

(3) The authority may deal with any number of separate pending applications, presented under section 15 in respect of persons belonging to the same unpaid group, as a single application presented under sub-section (2) of this section and the provisions of that sub-section shall apply accordingly.

Appeal

1. An appeal against an order dismissing either wholly or in part an application made under subsection (2) of section 15, or against a direction made under sub-section (3) or sub-section (4) of that section] may be preferred, within thirty days of the date on which the order or direction was made, in a Presidency-town before the Court of Small Causes and elsewhere before the District Court:

(*a*) by the employer or other person responsible for the payment of wages under section 3, if the total sum directed to be paid by way of wages and compensation exceeds three hundred rupees or such direction has the effect of imposing on the employer or the other person a financial liability exceeding one thousand rupees], or

(*b*) by an employed person on any legal practitioner or any official of a registered trade union authorised in writing to act on his behalf or any Inspector under this Act, or any other person permitted by the authority to make an application under sub-section (2) of section 15, if the total amount of wages claimed to have been withheld from the employed person exceeds twenty rupees or from the unpaid group to which the employed person belongs or belonged exceeds fifty rupees, or

(*c*) by any person directed to pay a penalty under 6*[sub-section (4)] of section 15.

(1A) No appeal under clause (a) of sub-section (1) shall lie unless the memorandum of appeal is accompanied by a certificate by the authority to the effect that the appellant has deposited the amount payable under the direction appealed against.

(2) Save as provided in sub-section (1), any order dismissing either wholly or in part an application made under sub-section (2) of section 15, or a direction made under sub-section (3) or sub-section (4) of that section shall be final.

(3) Where an employer prefers an appeal under this section, the authority against whose decision the appeal has been preferred may, and if so directed by the court referred to in sub-section (1) shall, pending the decision of the appeal, withhold payment of any sum in deposit with it.

(4) The court referred to in sub-section (1) may, if it thinks fit, submit any question of law for the decision of the High Court and, if it so does, shall decide the in conformity with such decision.

Conditional Attachment of Property of Employer or Other Persons Responsible for Payment of Wages

(1) Where at any time after an application has been made under sub-section (2) of section 15 the authority, or where at any time after an appeal has been filed under section 17 by an employed person or any legal practitioner or any official of a registered trade union authorised in writing to act on his behalf or any Inspector under this Act or any other person permitted by the authority to make an application under sub-section (2) of section 15 the Court referred to in that section, is satisfied that the employer or other person responsible for the payment of wages under section 3 is likely to evade payment of any amount that may be directed to be paid under section 15 or section 17, the authority or the Court, as the case may be, except in cases where the authority or Court is of opinion that the ends of justice would be defeated by the delay, after giving the employer or other person an opportunity of being heard, may direct the attachment of so much of the property of the employer or other person responsible the payment of wages as is, in the opinion of the authority or Court, sufficient to satisfy the amount which may be payable under the direction.

(2) The provisions of the Code of Civil Procedure, 1908, (5 of 1908) relating to attachment before judgment under that

Code shall, so far as may be, apply to any order for attachment under sub-section (1).

Powers of Authorities

Every authority appointed under sub-section (1) of section 15 shall have all the powers of a Civil Court under the Code of Civil Procedure, 1908 (5 of 1908), for the purpose of taking evidence and of enforcing the attendance of witnesses and compelling the production of documents and every such authority shall be deemed to be a Civil Court for all the purposes of section 195 and of Chapter XXVI of the Code of Criminal Procedure, 1973 (2 of 1974).

Power to recover from employer in certain cases.

Rep. by the Payment of Wages (Amendment) Act, 1964 (53 of 1964), s. 17(w.e.f. 1-2-1965).

Penalty for Offences Under the Act

1. Whoever being responsible for the payment of wages to an employed person contravenes any of the provisions of any of the following sections, namely, section 5 except sub-section (4) thereof, section 7, section 8 except sub-section (8) thereof, section 9, section 10 except subsection (2) thereof and sections 11 to 13, both inclusive, shall be punishable with fine 2*[which shall not be less than two hundred rupees but which may extend to one thousand rupees.

2. Whoever contravenes the provisions of section 4, sub-section (4) of section 5, section 6, subsection (8) of section 8, sub-section (2) of section 10] or section 25 shall be punishable with fine which may extend to five hundred rupees.

3. Whoever being required under this Act to maintain any records or registers or to furnish any information or return:

(*a*) fails to maintain such register or record; or

(*b*) wilfully refuses or without lawful excuse neglects to furnish such information or return; or

(*c*) wilfully furnishes or causes to be furnished any information or return which he knows to be false; or (*d*) refuses to answer or wilfully gives a false answer to any question necessary for obtaining any information required to be furnished under this Act; shall, for each such offence, be punishable with fine which shall not be less than two hundred rupees but which may extend to one thousand rupees,

Whoever-

(*a*) wilfully obstructs an Inspector in the discharge of his duties under this Act; or

(*b*) refuses or wilfully neglects to afford an Inspector any reasonable facility for making any entry, inspection, examination, supervision, or inquiry authorised by or under this Act in relation to any railway, factory or industrial or other establishment; or

(*c*) wilfully refuses to produce on the demand of an Inspector any register or other document kept in pursuance of this Act; or

(*d*) prevents or attempts to prevent or does anything which he has any reason to believe is likely to prevent any person from appearing before or being examined by an Inspector acting in pursuance of his duties under this Act; shall be punishable with fine which shall not be less than two hundred rupees but which may extend to one thousand rupees

5. If any person who has been convicted of any offence punishable under this Act is again guilty of an offence involving contravention of the same provision, he shall be punishable on a subsequent conviction with imprisonment for a term which shall not be less than one month but which may extend to six months and with fine which shall not be less than five hundred rupees but which may extend to three thousand rupees:

Provided that for the purpose of this sub-section, no cognizance shall be taken of any conviction made more than two years before the date on which the commission of the offence which is being punished came to the knowledge of the Inspector.

6. If any person fails or wilfully neglects to pay the wages of any employed person by the date fixed by the authority in this behalf, he shall, without prejudice to any other action that may be taken against him, be punishable with an additional fine which may extend to one hundred rupees for each day for which such failure or neglect continues.

Procedure in Trial of Offences

1. No Court shall take cognizance of a complaint against any person for an offence under subsection (1) of section 20 unless an application in respect of the facts constituting the offence has been presented under section 15 and has been granted wholly or in part and the authority empowered under the latter section or the appellate Court granting such application has sanctioned the making of the complaint.

2. Before sanctioning the making of a complaint against any person for an offence under sub-section (1) of section 20, the authority empowered under section 15 or the appellate Court, as the case may be, shall give such person an opportunity of showing cause against the granting of such sanction, and the sanction shall not be granted if such person satisfies the authority or Court that his default was due to:

(*a*) a bona fide error or bona fide dispute as to the amount payable to the employed person, or

(*b*) the occurrence of an emergency, or the existence of exceptional circumstances, such that the person responsible for the payment of the wages was unable, though exercising reasonable diligence, to make prompt payment, or

(*c*) the failure of the employed person to apply for or accept payment.

3. No Court shall take cognizance of a contravention of section 4 or of section 6 or of a contravention of any rule made under section 26 except on a complaint made by or with the sanction of an Inspector under this Act.

3A. No Court shall take congnizance of any offence punishable under sub-section (3) or sub-section (4) of section

20 except on a complaint made by or with the sanction of an Inspector under this Act.

4. In imposing any fine for an offence under sub-section (1) of section 20 the Court shall take into consideration the amount of any compensation already awarded against the accused in any proceedings taken under section 15

Bar of suits

No Court shall entertain any suit for the recovery of wages or of any deduction from wages in so far as the sum so claimed—

(*a*) forms the subject of an application under section IS which has been presented by the plaintiff and which is pending before the authority appointed under that section or of an appeal under section 17; or

(*b*) has formed the subject of a direction under section 15 in favour of the plaintiff; or

(*c*) has been adjudged, in any proceeding under section 15, to be owed to the plaintiff; or

(*d*) could have been recovered by an application under section 15.

Protection of action taken in good faith

No suit, prosecution or other legal proceeding shall lie against the Government or any officer of the Government for anything which is in good faith done or intended to be done under this Act.

Contracting out

Any contract or agreement, whether made before or after the commencement of this Act, whereby an employed person relinquishes any right conferred by this Act shall be null and void in so far as it purports to deprive him of such right.

Application of Act to Railways, Air Transport Services, Mines and Oilfields

The powers by this Act conferred upon the State Government shall, in relation to railways, air transport services, mines and oilfields, be powers of the Central Government.

Display by Notice of Abstracts of the Act

The person responsible for the payment of wages to persons employed in a factory or an industrial or other establishment] shall cause to be displayed in such factory or industrial or other establishment] a notice containing such abstracts of this Act and of the rules made there under in English and in the language of the majority of the persons employed in the factory or industrial or other establishment], as may be prescribed.

Payment of Undisturbed Wages in Cases of Death of Employed Person

1. Subject to the other provisions of the Act, all amounts payable to an employed person as wages shall, if such amounts could not or cannot be paid on account of his death before payment or on account of his whereabouts not being known—

   (*a*) be paid to the person nominated by him in this behalf in accordance with the rules made under this Act; or

   (*b*) where no such nomination has been made or where for any reasons such amounts cannot be paid to the person so nominated, be deposited with the prescribed authority who shall deal with the amounts so deposited in such manner as may be prescribed.

2. Where, in accordance with the provisions of sub-section (1), all amounts payable to an employed person as wages—

   (*a*) are paid by the employer to the person nominated by the employed person; or

   (*b*) are deposited by the employer with the prescribed authority, the employer shall be discharged of his liability to pay those wages.

Rule-making power

1. The State Government may make rules to regulate the procedure to be followed by the authorities and Courts referred to in sections 15 and 17.

2. The State Government may, by notification in the Official Gazette, make rules for the purpose of carrying into effect the provisions of this Act.

3. In particular and without prejudice to the generality of the foregoing power, rules made under sub-section (2) may—

(*a*) require the maintenance of such records, registers and notices as are necessary for the enforcement of the Act prescribe the form thereof and the particulars to be entered in such registers or records;

(*b*) require the display in a conspicuous place on premises where employment is carried on of notices specifying rates of wages payable to persons employed on such premises;

(*c*) provide for the regular inspection of the weights, and weighing machines used by employers in checking or ascertaining the wages of persons employed by them;

(*d*) prescribe the manner of giving notice of the days on which wages will be paid;

(*e*) prescribe the authority competent to approve under sub-section (1) of section 8 acts and omissions in respect of which fines may be imposed;

(*f*) prescribe the procedure for the imposition of fines under section 8 and for the making of the deductions referred to in section 10;

(*g*) prescribe the conditions subject to which deductions may be made under the proviso to sub-section (2) of section 9;

(*h*) prescribe the authority competent to approve the purposes on which the proceeds of fines shall be expended;

(*i*) prescribe the extent to which advances may be made and the instalments by which they may be recovered with reference to clause (b) of section 12;

(*ia*) prescribe the extent to which loans may be granted and the rate of interest payable thereon with reference to section 12A;

(*ib*) prescribe the powers of Inspectors for the purposes of this Act;

(*j*) regulate the scales of costs which may be allowed in proceedings under this Act;

(*k*) prescribe the amount of court-fees payable in respect of any proceedings under this Act, 2;

(*l*) prescribe the abstracts to be contained in the notices required by section 25;

(*la*) prescribe the form and manner in which nominations may be made for the purposes of sub-section (1) of section 25A, the cancellation or variation of any such nomination, or the making of any fresh nomination in the event of the nominee predeceasing the person making nomination, and other matters connected with such nominations;

(*lb*) specify the authority with whom amounts required to be deposited under clause (b) of sub-section (1) of section 25A shall be deposited, and the manner in which such authority shall deal with the amounts deposited with it under that clause;]

(*m*) provide for any other matter which is to be or may be prescribed.

4. In making any rule under this section the State Government may provide that a contravention of the rule shall be punishable with fine which may extend to two hundred rupees.

5. All rules made under this section shall be subject to the condition of previous publication and the date to be specified under clause (3) of section 23 of the General Clauses Act, 1897 (10 of 1897), shall not be less than three months from the date on which the draft of the proposed rules was published.

6. Every rule made by the Central Government under this section shall be laid, as soon as may be after it is made, before each House of Parliament while it is in session for a total period of thirty days which may be comprised in one session or in two or more successive sessions and if, before the expiry of the session immediately following the session or the successive sessions aforesaid, both Houses agree in making any modification in the rule, or both Houses agree that the rule should not be made, the rule shall thereafter have effect only

in such modified form or be of no effect, as the case may be; so, however, that any such modification or annulment shall be without prejudice to the validity of anything previously done under that rule.

Pay Commission

The Pay Commission is an administrative system/mechanism that the government of India [*Images*] set up in 1956 to determine the salaries of government employees. A Pay Commission is a panel of members of the *Union Cabinet of India* for raising the salaries of government employees.

The First Pay Commission was established in 1956 and since then, every decade has seen the birth of a commission that decides the wages of government employees for a particular time-frame.

The Second Pay Commission was set up in August 1957 and gave its report in two years. The third Pay Commission, set up in April 1970, submitted its report in March 1973.

The recommendations of the Fourth Pay Commission covered the period between 1986 and 1996. The Fifth Pay Commission covered the period between 1996 and this year.

The Union Cabinet, under the stewardship of Prime Minister Manmohan Singh, approved the setting up of the 6th Pay Commission to revise the payscales of central government employees in July 2006.

The 6th Pay Commission is headed by its Chairman Justice B N Srikrishna, and has Ravindra Dholakia, J S Mathur and Sushama Nath as its other members.

The Pay Commission was supposed to submit its report in 18 months.

The 7th Pay Commission is about submit its report very soon.

CHAPTER

6 Job Evaluation

Definition

According to Edwin B. Flippo, "Job evaluation is a systematic and orderly process of determining the worth of job in relation to other jobs".

Job evaluation means determining the relative worth of a job in an organization by comparing it with other jobs within an organization and with job market outside jobs are evaluated on the basis of their content and are placed in the order of their importance. In this way, job evaluation helps in establishing job hierarchy. It is a process by which jobs in an organization are appraised. It suggests comparative importance of different jobs. A wage structure hierarchy is based on such job evaluation.

In job evaluation the jobs are ranked on the basis of their relative importance and not the job holders. They are rated through performance appraisal. Job evaluation is the output provided through job analysis.

Features

1. It determines the relative worth of jobs in an organization. Jobs are evaluated as per their content and place in the order of their importance.
2. It is based on the analysis of the facts about the job collected through job analysis.
3. It helps to bring a balanced wage structure in an organization. This is possible as job hierarchy is established. The purpose is fixation of satisfactory wage differentials among various jobs.

Objectives

1. To establish by impartial judgement the logical and accurate relationship of each job to other jobs within the firm.
2. To establish satisfactory wage and salary differentials.
3. To select employees more accurately and train, promote or transfer them within the firm objectively and impartially.
4. To provide them information for work organization, employees selection, placement and other similar problems.
5. To promote employee goodwill, strengthen and maintain morale and loyalty and provide an incentive for efficiency.
6. To determine the rate of pay for each job that is fair and equitable in relation to other jobs in the plant.

Advantages/Importance

1. Job evaluation clearly indicates the relative worth of different jobs in the organization.
2. It establishes a hierarchy of jobs and evolves a graduated wage scale for employees.
3. It is useful for introducing a satisfactory, rational and balanced wage structure in an organization. It is also useful for simplifying wage administration.
4. It promotes employees goodwill, strengthens and maintains high morale and loyalty of workers and also provides incentives for raising efficiency.
5. It provides a scientific base for promotions and transfers of workers in an organization.
6. It avoids injustice to workers as regards wage payment, promotions and transfers.
7. It simplifies wage administration and facilitates merit rating and training programmes for employees.
8. It removes grievances and disputes among employees over relative wages and makes the wage system acceptable to all employees.

Methods of Job Evaluation

1. *The ranking or granding method:* This method is considered to be the simplest and the last formal of all the job evaluation methods. Here the aim is to judge the job as a whole and determine its relative value by ranking one whole job as against another whole job. Under this method, the jobs are arranged in order to their importance with the most important job at the highest end and the least important job at the lowest end. The remaining jobs are arranged as per their relative importance through suitable evaluation techniques. The ranking is conducted through a committee of experts' job raters. The committee is supplied with the necessary information (job description and job specification) for the ranking of available jobs. The ranking is done at the departmental level and for every department, the jobs are ranked I order of importance. This creates a hierarchy of jobs within the department. In this method which is non analytical, the ranking of jobs is based on the nature and importance of the job, responsibilities involved, qualities and qualifications required and the working conditions connected with the job.

Advantages

1. Simplicity - it is easily understood to all the concerned and also to operate/administer.
2. It is inexpensive.
3. It can be used conveniently in small establishments.

Disadvantages

1. It does not indicate the degree of difference between the jobs. It merely shows that one job is more or less important than other job.
2. In most cases, the rankings are not based on job description but on the rater's general knowledge of the jobs.
3. It is complex for a large firm with a complex organization structure.

2. *The factor comparison or weight in money method:* It is an analytical method. The rating process consists of delineation

of common key factors of different jobs and assessment of monetary values thereto with a view to assessing their relative worth on the basis of sum total of the monetary values. Job description provides the data required for indicating the major job elements or factors found in greater or lesser degree in the activities of the entire enterprise.

It is a qualitative method of job rating involving complicated procedure. As a result, the services of experts are required for actual job rating.

This method begins by selecting the crucial or critical components or elements characterizing the business operations of the firm. In other words, a schedule of job factors is drawn up by careful analysis of the operations.

The factors under this method are:

1. Mental requirements
2. Skill requirements
3. Physical requirements
4. Responsibility range
5. Working conditions.

After the key elements are selected/for analyzing the jobs, the weights are applied tot job elements. Assessment of weights is done by an expert committee. As per such weights, the jobs are ranked. A monetary value is assigned to each factor of all jobs. All these values of individual jobs are weighted and then the total value of each job is arrived at or is readily available.

Advantages

1. It is more accurate and systematic than the simple ranking method. The dissimilar jobs can be rated on the basis of common factors.
2. The services of experts are used and this makes the system realistic and accurate.

Disadvantages

1. It is complicated, expensive, laborious and not easily explainable to employees.

2. Application of weightages and monetary values may involve the bias of experts.
3. This method is difficult to install and is not used extensively.

3. *The point rating method:* This method is one popular and extensively used method of job evaluation. In this method, each job is evaluated separately, appraising each of the factors such as skill, effort, responsibility and working conditions and combining the separate evaluations into a single point score for each job. In this method a series of rating scales is constructed one for each of the factors which have been selected as important in the work of the position. A certain number of points are allowed for each scale. In this way, differences among jobs are reflected in the different values which are assigned to the factors. By the use of point rating method, each job is reduced to a numerical value so that similarity and differences in work and difficulty are discovered.

The straight point system in which each factor has the same number of degrees and corresponding points is indicated in the following chart:

Factors	Degrees				
	1	2	3	4	5
Education	10	20	30	40	50
Experience	10	20	30	40	50
Physical Demand	10	20	30	40	50
Responsibility for Process	10	20	30	40	50
Responsibility for Safety	10	20	30	40	50
Responsibility for Materials	10	20	30	40	50
Working Conditions	10	20	30	40	50
Hazards	10	20	30	40	50

The weighted point system the number of degrees is shown in the chart given below:

Factors	Degrees				
	1	2	3	4	5
Education	10	20	30	40	50
Experience	30	60	90	120	150
Physical Demand	20	40	60	80	100
Responsibility for Process	10	20	30	40	60
Responsibility for Safety	5	10	15	20	25
Responsibility for Materials	10	20	30	40	50
Working Conditions	10	20	30	40	50
Hazards	5	10	15	20	25

Advantages

1. This method is analytical in its approach.
2. It gives a quantitative value for each job. This makes it easy to explain to a worker who has some doubt in his mind about the absolute and relative wages fixed for his job.
3. The outstanding feature of this method is the use of a manual. Basis and guidelines of valuation are standardized by experts and are codified in this manual.

Limitations

1. This method may suffer from inequities if listing and weighting of points are defective due to indifference on the part of rater.
2. The manual used for ranking the jobs needs periodical revision. If not revised it may become outmoded and evaluation based thereon would be out of tune with the changed trends.
3. It is difficult for application and may prove to be unintelligible to the workers.

CHAPTER

7 Wage Payment System

Introduction

Wage is a monetary payment made by the employer to his employee for the work done or services rendered. It is a monetary compensation for the services rendered. A worker may be paid ₹ 100 per day or ₹ 4500 per month. This is wage payment. The worker gives his services and takes payment called wage payment. Industrial workers are paid remuneration for their services in terms of money called wage payment. Wages are usually paid in cash at the end of one day, one month or one week. Money wage is the monetary compensation or price paid by the employer to his employee for the services rendered. Such compensation is also called wage or salary or reward given by an organisation to a person in return to a work done.

Generally, compensation payable to an employee includes the following three components:

- Basic compensation for the job (wage/salary)
- Incentive compensation for the employee on job
- Supplementary compensation paid to employees (fringe benefit and employee services)

Importance of Wage Payment

1. *To worker:* Wage payment is important to all categories of workers. Wage is a matter of fife and death to workers/ employees. Their life, welfare and even social status depend on wage payment. It is only source of income to large majority of workers. They and their unions always demand higher.wages and other monetary benefits.

Majority of labour problems and disputes are directly related to wage payment. The efficiency of workers and their interest and involvement in the work depend on wage payment. Even their attitude towards employer depends on wage payment. In brief, wage payment is a matter of greatest importance to workers. Wage problem is the most pressing and persistent problem before the entire labour force.

2. *To employer:* Wage payment is equally important to employers as their profit depend on the total wage bill. An employer in general is interested in paying low wages and thereby controls the cost of production. However, low wages are not necessarily economical. In fact they may prove to be too costly to the employer in the long run, e.g. In garment manufacturing company if tailors are not paid properly then it is difficult for the company to retain them. An employer has a moral and social responsibility to pay fair wages to his worker as they are equal partners in the production process. He should give fair wages which will benefit to both the parties. Employees will offer full co-operation to the management when they are paid attractive wages. On the other hand, strikes and disputes are likely to develop when workers are paid low wages or when they are dissatisfied and angry due to low wage rates. It is possible to earn more profit by paying attractive wages to workers, e.g. Reliance, Citi Bank, Motorola are earned huge profits because of their higher pay packages.

3. *To government:* Government also give special importance and attention to wages paid to industrial workers as industrial development, productivity, industrial peace and cordial labour-management relation depend on the wage payment to workers. Government desires to give protection to the working class and for this minimum wages act and other Acts are made. In India, wages are now link with the cost of living. This is for the protection of workers. Government is the biggest employer in India and the wage rates of government servant and employees of public sector organisations are decided by government only. Revision of pay scale of government employees made for adjusting their wages as per the cost of living. For this, "Pay

Commission" is appointed and pay scale is adjusted as per the recommendations made.

In India, wage payment is very critical, controversial and delicate issue for all categories of work force. This is due to poverty, rising prices, mass unemployment and rising population. Wage payment indeed a vexatious problem and needs to be tackled from economic, social and humanistic angles.

Concept of Fair Wages

Fair wages is the wage which is above the minimum wage but below the living wage. Obviously the lower limit of the fair wage is the minimum wage and the upper limit is set by the ability of the industry to pay. Between these two limits, fair wages should depend on the factors like:

1. Prevailing rates of wages in the same occupation
2. Prevailing rates of wages in the same region or neighbouring areas
3. Employers ability to pay
4. Level of national income and its distribution
5. Productivity of labour
6. Status enjoyed by the industry in the economy.

Hence it can be said that fair wages are determined on industry cum region basis. When fair wages are paid employees enjoy higher standard of living. It is accepted fact that wages must be fair and reasonable. Wages is fair when the employee is able to meet its essential needs and enjoy reasonable standard of living. "Equal pay for equal work" serves as base of fair wage.

According to *Encyclopaedia of Social Science*, "Fair wages are equal to those received by the workers performing work of equal skill, difficulty or unpleasantness."

Factors Influencing Wage and Salary Structure

- *The organization's ability to pay:* Wage increases should be given by those organizations which can afford them. Companies that have good sales and therefore high profits tend to pay higher wages than those which are running at a loss or earning low profits because of the high cost of production or low sales.

- *Supply and demand of labour:* If the demand and certain skills are high and the supply is low the result is rise in the price to be paid for these skills. The other alternative is to pay higher wages if the labour supply is scarce and lower wages when it is excessive.
- *The cost of living:* When the cost of living increases, workers.and trade unions demand adjusted wages to offset the erosion of real wages. However when living costs are stable or decline the management does not resort with this argument as a reason for wage reduction.
- *The living wage:* Employers feel that the level of living prescribed in workers budget is opened to argument since it is based on subjective opinion.
- *Job requirements:* Jobs are graded according to the relative skill responsibility and job conditions required.
- *Trade unions bargaining power:* Trade unions do affect the rate of wages. Generally the stronger and more powerful trade union, higher the wages.
- *Productivity:* Productivity is another criterion and is measured in terms of output man-hour. It is not due to labour efforts alone. Technological improvements, greater ingenuity and skill by the labour are all responsible for the increase in productivity.
- *Prevailing market rate:* This is also known as 'comparable wages' or 'going wage rate'. Reason behind this is competition demand that competitors adhere to the same relative wage level.
- *Skill levels available in the market:* With the rapid growth of industries, business trade there is shortage of skilled resources. The technological development, automation has been affecting the skilled levels at a faster rate.
- *Psychological and social factors:* This determine in a significant measure how hard a person will work for the compensation received or what pressures he will exert to get his compensation increased.

Components of Employee Remuneration

The remuneration packet of an employee includes wage/salary, incentives, fringe benefits, perquisites and finally non-monetary benefits.

This is made clear in the following chart:

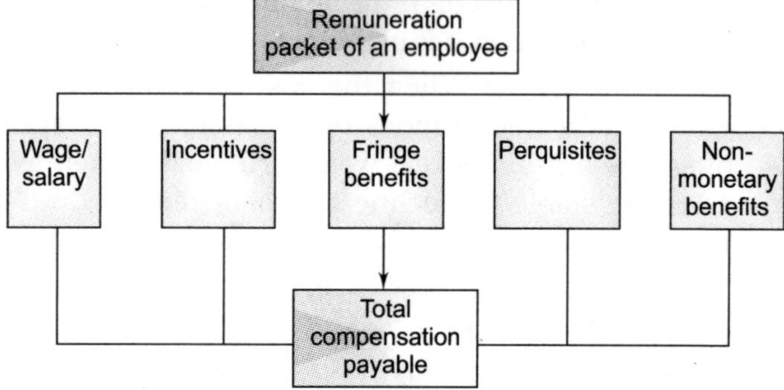

1. *Wages and salary:* Wages represent hourly rates of pay, and salary refers to the monthly rate of pay, irrespective of the number of hours put in by the employee. Wages and salaries are subject to the annual increments. They differ from employee to employee and depend upon the nature of job, seniority and merit.

2. *Incentives:* Incentives are paid in addition to wages and salaries and are also called 'payments by results'. Incentives depend upon productivity, sales, profit, or cost reduction efforts.

There are: (*a*) Individual incentive schemes, and (*b*) Group incentive programmes. Individual incentives are applicable to specific employee performance. Where a given task demands group efforts for completion, incentives are paid to the group as a whole. The amount is later divided among group members on an equitable basis.

3. *Fringe benefits:* These are monetary benefits provided to employees. They include the benefit of: (*a*) Provident fund, (*b*) Gratuity, (*c*) Medical care, (*d*) Hospitalization payment, (*e*) Accident relief, (*f*) Health and Group insurance, (*g*) Subsidized canteen facilities, (*h*) Recreational facilities, and (*i*) Provision of uniforms to employees.

4. *Perquisites:* There are special benefits offered to managers/ executives. The purpose is to retain competent executives. Perquisites include the following: (*a*) Company car for traveling, (*b*) Club membership, (*c*) Paid holidays, (*d*) Furnished house or accommodation, (*e*) Stock option schemes, etc.

5. *Non-monetary benefits:* These benefits give psychological satisfaction to employees even when financial benefit is not available. Such benefits are: (*a*) Recognition of merit through certificate, etc. (*b*) Offering challenging job responsibilities, (*c*) Promoting growth prospects, (*d*) Comfortable working conditions, (*e*) Competent supervision, and (*f*) Job sharing and flexi-time.

Systems of Wage Payment

A. Time Rate System

B. Piece Rate System

Time Rate System

It is the oldest and simplest method of wage payment used extensively in the industrial as well as government departments. Wages are paid as per the time spent by the workers in the factory. The production given by them is not taken into consideration. The employer buys the hours of the workers and pays them accordingly. Time rate system is also called as day wage system. In the time rate system, efficiency, sincerity, ability is not given attention and all the workers are paid at one and the same rate as per the period spent in the factory.

Advantages of Time Rate System

1. *Easy and simple:* Time rate is easy to understand and simple to follow and calculate. Wage calculations are also easy and quick. Each worker knows how much wage payment he is entitled to at the end of the month. This gives convenience to employer and employees.
2. *Guarantee of minimum wage:* It gives the guarantee of certain minimum wage payment to every worker irrespective of their working capacity. Workers get

a regular and stable income and this gives a sense of security to all workers as regards wage payment.

3. *Maintains duality of production:* Quality of production is maintained here as the workers are not in a hurry to complete the work. They do not rush the job and spoil the quality because of the temptation to earn more. Workers tend to work slowly and with care. Even accidents are less as workers use the machines in a careful manner.
4. *Support from trade unions:* Workers and trade unions accept and support time rate system as all workers are placed in one category as regards wage payment. This ensures unity among workers. Trade unions normally prefer time rate system of wage payment.
5. *Avoids quarrels among workers:* Time rate avoids heart burning and quarrels among the workers as uniform wages are paid to all. Here efficiency, honesty and sincerity of workers are not given any special weightage. Wage rate is the same for sincere and lazy workers.
6. *Convenient in modern factory system:* Time rate payment is convenient in modern factory system where production process is continuous and integrated. It is not possible to measure the work completed by one individual worker and hence time rate system is convenient.

Disadvantages of Time Rate System

1. *Not scientific:* Time rate is not scientific system of wage payment as there is no direct linking between wages and production/productivity. Wages bill may increase without corresponding increase in the production. This will bring loss to the employer/management.
2. *Absence of positive encouragement:* In the time rate system, there is no positive encouragement to workers to improve their efficiency/performance as the wage rate is uniform to all workers; efficient and inefficient.
3. *No distinction between workers:* In the time rate system no distinction is made between efficient and lazy workers,

both are paid at one rate which is unfair. This system gives punishment to sincere and efficient workers. They are discouraged as they are paid less than what they deserve. They may even leave the job.

4. *No initiative to workers:* Time rate fails to encourage workers to take more interest and initiative in their work. In fact, it encourages them to follow "go slow" policy. This is because wage payment is not linked with the production given.
5. *Labour cost may increase:* In the time rate system, there is a possibility of increase in the labour cost without corresponding increase in the production. Workers may work with slow speed, give less production but collect the wage as per time or day fixed.
6. *Strict supervision:* In the time rate strict supervision on the workers is essential as payment is for period and not production. This raises the expenditure on supervision.
7. *No effect on productivity/ efficiency:* Time rate fails to raise productivity and efficiency of labour force. It is not an incentive system of wage payment.

Piece Rate System

This is another basic system of wage payment. It is just opposite to the time rate. It is also treated as an incentive wage system as it encourages workers to produce more and also to earn more. In the piece rate system, wages are paid as per the output or production given by the worker and not as per the time spent by the worker in the factory. Payment is by results in terms of output given. Wage rate is fixed per piece of work or for certain quantity of production. The production given by a worker at the end of the day is counted and payment is made accordingly.

Merits/Advantages of Piece Rate System

1. *Linking of wages with production:* Here wages are linked with production or productivity. It raises the productivity of labour. Workers work with speed and use their capacity fully as the wage payment is

directly related to the quantity of production given by a worker.

2. *Distinction is made between efficient and inefficient workers:* Distinction is made between efficient and inefficient worker and full justice is done to efficient worker as he gets payment in proportion to the production given. Efficient workers support the piece rate system but it is not preferred by unskilled and inefficient workers. They get less payment under this method as their capacity to produce is less.
3. *Encourages workers to take initiative in the work:* Piece rate system encourages workers to take more interest and initiative in the work as every worker gets full reward of his efforts. There is direct efforts-reward relationship in the piece rate system.
4. *Fair to employer and employees:* This system is fair to employers as well as employees. The employees get income in proportion to production given by them and the employer gets production in proportion to the wage paid.
5. *Incentive system:* This system serves as the incentive system. Workers work efficiently and take interest in the work due to corresponding benefit/reward in the form of higher wage payment.
6. *Limited supervision adequate:* In this system strict supervision on the workers is not necessary as workers work sincerely. This is because their wage payment is directly linked with their sincerity and ability.
7. *Freedom of work to workers:* Workers get more freedom of work and there is effective control on the cost of production in the piece rate system.
8. *Brings cordial relations:* Piece rate brings cordial labour-management relations and industrial peace.

Demerits/Limitation of Piece Rate System

1. *No guarantee of minimum wage payment:* There is no guarantee of certain minimum wage payment to a

worker. This may prove to be dangerous particularly to a newly recruited worker and workers who are below average.

2. *Workers suffer even when they are not at fault:* Sometimes workers suffer in wage payment even when they are not fault. Due to power failure, etc. they may not be able to give production and naturally they will not be eligible for wage payment even when they remain present in the factory for the whole day.
3. *Complicated system:* Piece rate system is complicated and difficult as it is difficult to understand by ordinary workers. Management will have to keep elaborate records of production given by each worker. Workers also make complaints as regards wage payment when they feel that due payment is not made to them.
4. *Disturbs unity of workers:* Piece rate affects the unity among workers as wage payment will not be uniform to all workers. This will lead to quarrel among workers. Trade unions oppose piece rate system on the ground that it will lead to rivalry among workers and destroy unity among them.
5. *Not fair to trainees:* Piece rate system is not fair to trainees, as their capacity to produce is less and naturally they will get less wages.
6. *Quality of production is adversely affected:* It affects the quality of production as workers may work with speed and this may bring down the quality of production. In addition the wastages and spoiled work are likely to increase due to haste on the part of the workers to labour hard and over strain themselves in order to earn more. This affects the health of workers.

Time Rate v/s Piece Rate Systemsi

Time Rate	Piece Rate
Meaning: Wages are paid as per the time spent by workers.	Wages are paid as per the output or production given by workers.

Old/new svstem: Oldest and simplest method of wage payment.	Modern and incentive system of wage system.
Guarantee of wages: Gives guarantee of certain minimum wage payment to every worker.	Fails to give guarantee of minimum wage payment to every worker.
Support: Employees and trade unions support time rate system.	Employers and efficient workers prefer piece rate system.
Understanding of system: Easy to understand and simple to administer.	Complicated system as various recorded and registers are required to be maintained
Distinction between workers: Distinction is not made between efficient and inefficient workers as all are paid at one and same rate.	Distinction is made between efficient and inefficient workers. Efficient worker is paid more while an inefficient worker is paid less.
Effect on production: Encourages workers to follow go-slow policy and naturally production suffers.	Encourages workers to take more interest in the work and naturally production increases.
Quality of production: Quality, workmanship of production are not affected, raw materials, machinery are utilised properly. The spoiled work is also negligible.	Quality, workmanship of production may suffer. Increase in spoiled work and wastage of raw materials.
Supervision: Strict supervision is necessary as workers are paid as per the period spent.	Strict supervision is not necessary as workers are paid in proportion to the production given.
Suitability: Suitable to manufacturing units, also suitable when individual contribution is not easily measurable.	Suitable when contribution of individual worker is measurable and work is standardised and repitive in character.

Incentive of Wage Payment

The wage plan should be highly incentive means it should encourage workers to take more initiative and interest in the work, produce more and also earn more. The wage plan which serves all these purposes is called incentive wage plan. Such an incentive plan is beneficial to both - employers and employees as well as it is useful for the rapid industrial growth.

Incentives include monetary as weft as non-monetary benefits offered. There is motivation to work hard and to earn more. In every incentive plan, wages are linked with the given output. Incentives are not fixed like wages and salaries. They vary from individual to individual and from period to period.

ILO defines incentives as "payment by results". Incentives can also be described as "incentive systems of payment".

According to Dale Yoder, "Incentive wages relate earnings to productivity and may use premiums, bonuses, or a variety of rates to compensate for superior performance" Piece rate system is the oldest incentive wage plan which is also useful for attracting and retaining qualified personnel in the organisation and for motivating personnel to higher levels of performance. In many incentive plans, a combination of time rate and piece rate systems is used. Such combination creates an ideal incentive plan.

Types of Incentive Plans

There are two types of incentive plans:

(*a*) Individual incentive plans, and

(*b*) Group incentive plans.

Individual incentive plan is meant for individual employees. He has to work hard i.e. efficiently, produce more and share the monetary benefits for himself. The benefit is directly linked with his ability, efficiency and capacity.

In the group incentive plan, the incentive is not for individual employee but for the group of employees working in one department or section. Such group incentive plan may cover the entire labour force of a production unit. The group will work collectively, give more production and share the benefit. Initially the benefit will be given to the group and thereafter, it will be divided among the members of the group.

Management is interested in group incentive plan while employees are interested in individual incentive plans. Production activities are now conducted in an integrated manner and naturally incentives should be offered to the employees. Group incentive plans are better as they encourage team spirit and develop cooperation and understanding among the employees. This avoids wastages and promotes productivity.

FEATURES/REQUISITES OF A GOOD INCENTIVE PLAN

Simplicity

A good incentive plan is one which is easy to understand and simple to operate. An average worker must be able to know the incentive offered and what he is expected to do. The monetary as well as non-monetary benefits offered must be made clear to all workers.

Encourage Initiative

A good incentive plan should create initiative among workers to work more and to earn more. It must offer more income to workers and more profit/production to the firm or company.

Definiteness and Flexibility

A good incentive plan should be definite. This means frequent changes should not be made as regard rates, etc. as such changes create confusion and doubts in the minds of workers. Such plan must give clear benefits to workers

In addition, an ideal incentive plan should be flexible. It should take care of technological and other changes taking place from time-to-time. There should be suitable provision for such adjustment. Flexibility makes incentive plan adaptable.

Wide Coverage and Equitable

A good incentive plan should not be for employees in certain departments only. It should have a wide coverage and almost all employees should be covered in such plan. Such wide coverage makes the plan popular at all levels and among all categories of workers.

An incentive plan should be equitable. This means it should provide equal opportunity to all employees to show efficiency and earn more. This avoids dissatisfaction among employees and makes the plan just and fair to all employees.

Guarantee of Minimum Wage Payment

An incentive wage plan should include certain minimum wage payment to every worker per month. This should be irrespective of the production he gives. Such provision of guarantee payments creates a sense of security and confidence among workers.

Scientific Fixation of Standard Workload

Under the incentive plan, extra payment is given for the extra work i.e. work which is over and above certain quality. Such standard work-load must be clear, specific and fixed with scientific time studies so that majority of employees will be able to give extra production for extra payment.

Justice to Employer and Employees

A good incentive plan should do justice to both parties. The employer must get additional production along with extra profit and the workers must get extra payment for extra production.

PROFIT-SHARING

Profit-sharing is regarded as a steppingstone to industrial democracy. Prof. Seager observes: "Profit-sharing is an agreement by which employees receive a share, fixed in advance of the profits."

Profit-sharing usually involves the determination of an organisation's profit at the end of the fiscal year and the distribution of a percentage of the profits to the workers qualified to share in the earnings. The percentage to be shared by the workers is often predetermined at the beginning of the work period and IS often communicated to the workers so that they have some knowledge of their potential gains. To enable the workers to participate in profit-sharing, they are required to work for certain number of years and develop some seniority. The theory behind profit-sharing is that management feels its workers will fulfil their responsibilities more diligently if they realise that their efforts may result in higher profits, which will be returned to the workers through profit-sharing.

FEATURES OF PROFIT-SHARING

The main features of the profit-sharing schemes are:

(*a*) The agreement is voluntary and based on joint consultation made freely between the employers and the employees.

(*b*) The payment may be in form of cash, stock of future credits of some amount over and above the normal remuneration that would otherwise be paid to employees in a given situation.

(*c*) The employees should have some minimum qualifications, such as tenure or satisfy some other conditions of the service which may be determined by the management.

(*d*) The amount to be distributed among the participants is computed on the basis of some agreed formula, which is to be applied in all circumstances.

(*e*) The amount to be distributed depends on the price earned by the enterprise.

(*f*) The proportion of the profits distributed among the employees is determined in advance.

Objectives of Profit-sharing

1. To supplement the regular earning of trie workers,
2. To create a sense of partnership among the workers and the management,
3. To enable the workers to participate in the prosperity of their company,
4. To develop cordial labour-management relations and to improve employee morale,
5. To introduce incentive wage plan,
6. To raise productive efficiency by reducing costs and increasing output,
7. To reduce labour turnover and to improve public relations,
8. To provide for employee security in the event of death, retirement or disability.

ADVANTAGES OF PROFIT-SHARING

1. *Extra income to workers:* Workers get extra cash payment due to profit-sharing arrangement. This money is useful for raising their welfare. Workers can purchase costly consumer durables out of this money available at one time. Thus, profit-sharing

provides better life and welfare to workers. It creates contended labour force with higher standard of living. Profit-sharing plan acts as a good supplement to regular wages paid to employees. In fact, profit-sharing is aptly described as a form of *added remuneration.*

2. *Workers take more initiative and interest in the work:* Due to profit-sharing arrangement, workers/employees take more interest in the work. This develops team spirit among the employees because their share in the profit depends on their collective initiative, efforts and hard work. In this sense, profit-sharing is useful for motivating employees. It encourages employees to be regular, stable and efficient as the benefits of these elements are offered to them through profit-sharing. Here, efforts and reward are directly and proportionately linked. This encourages employees to take keen interest in the work and develops team spirit.

Profit-sharing acts not only as supplement to regular wages (i.e. as an incentive wage plan) but also as a motivating factor to all employees. It creates common objective before employer and employees and diverts their energies for achieving one common objective.

3. *Increase in production and productivity:* Profit-sharing acts as a driving force for more production and productivity. It motivates workers for raising production as they get direct and immediate benefit of additional efforts on their part. The benefits of increase in production are available to employer and employees.

4. *Fair to employer and emplovees:* Profit-sharing gives mere remuneration to workers along with more profit to employer. Employer pays a part of profit to workers but he is not adversely affected as profit is paid only when it exceeds a particular limit agreed by both the parties. This arrangement is, certainly fair to both parties. There is an element of social justice in it.

5. *Ensures cordial industrial relations:* Profit-sharing creates cordial labour-management relations. It. reduces industrial disputes, strikes and lock-outs. This is because both have

common objective and both are likely to suffer due to industrial disputes, strikes and lock-outs. Thus, profit-sharing reduces industrial disputes and leads to friendly relations between employer and employees. It certainly acts as a tool for reducing industrial disputes and also for creating industrial peace.

Thus, profit-sharing agreement encourages workers to work efficiently and also avoid dispute and quarrels with the employer. It acts as a natural and self-imposed check on industrial disputes. Profit-sharing creates team spirit in the higher cadres of management as well as in the rank and file of workers.

7. *Less supervision required:* Profit-sharing reduces the expenditure on supervision of workers as they take interest in the work on their own. Moreover, wastage of materials, volume of spoiled work, etc. are also reduced.

7. *Stability to labour force:* Profit-sharing brings stability to labour force as the benefit of profit-sharing is usually given only to those who work in the company for the whole year. Thus, profit-sharing brings down the rate of labour turnover and this gives benefit to the employer/management.

8. *Promotes social justice:* Profit-sharing is a method of social justice. It is a method by which workers are given the reward of their hard work and also allowed to participate in the progress and prosperity of their company. Profit-sharing introduces industrial democracy as workers are treated not only as wage earners but also as partners for sharing the profits of the company.

Disadvantages of Profit-sharing

1. *Uncertainty:* There is high degree of uncertainty in the profit-sharing scheme/plan. Profit-sharing is uncertain because it will be paid only when the profit exceeds a particular limit. The profit may not cross a particular limit due to market forces and the workers will suffer. Thus, profit-sharing does not give full guarantee of extra payment to workers. It acts like a fair weather plan.

2. *Unfair to efficient workers:* Profit-sharing is a group incentive plan. It gives equal benefit to all workers. Distinction is not made between good and bad workers. As a result sincere and efficient workers get less than what they deserve while insincere and inefficient get more than what they deserve.

3. *Opposition from trade unions:* Trade unions and workers feel that bonus payment is better than profit-sharing. They generally oppose to profit-sharing and demand bonus from the employer as it is a cheap alternative to profit-sharing.

4. *Disputes on calculation of net profit:* In profit-sharing, the net profit is to be calculated at the end of the financial year. There is a possibility of difficulties as regards the calculation of the net profit. The employer may like to manipulate the accounts and show less profit while workers may calculate it as high. Such quarrel affects both the parties as it leads to dispute and delay in payment. In brief, ascertaining net profits is one sensitive problem in profit-sharing.

5. *Adverse effects on labour-management relations:* Sometimes, relations between labour and management are adversely affected on the point of profit-sharing agreement. This defeats the very purpose of profit-sharing. Disputes are possible as regards the profit-sharing agreement itself.

6. *Not useful during depression:* Profit-sharing as a method of extra remuneration to workers can be used during the period of prosperity when profits are high. It cannot be used during the years of depression. Even newly established companies are not in a position to introduce profit-sharing scheme for their employees.

7. *Opposition from conservative employers:* The concept of profit-sharing is not fully acceptable to conservative employers. They feel that profit is the reward for the risks and uncertainties. They also argue that workers must be prepared to share profit as well as loss in the business.

FRINGE BENEFITS

Fringe benefits may be defined as wide range of benefits and services that employees receive as an integral part of their total compensation package. They are based on critical job factors and performance. Fringe benefits constitute indirect compensation as they are usually extended as a condition of employment and not directly related to performance of concerned employee. Fringe benefits are supplements to regular wages received by the workers at a cost of employers. They include benefits such as paid vacation, pension, health and insurance plans, etc. Such benefits are computable in terms of money and the amount of benefit is generally not predetermined.

The purpose of fringe benefits is to retain efficient and capable people in the organisation over a long period. They foster loyalty and acts as a security base for the employees.

Features of Fringe Benefits

- *Different from regular wages:* Fringe benefits are different from regular wages as such benefits are those payments, which an employee enjoys in addition to wages he receives. It is a supplementary payment and provides support to an employee.
- *Employee motivation:* Fringe benefits are not given to employees for performing certain jobs. The purpose is to encourage them to take more interest in the assigned work.
- *Useful but avoidable expenditure:* Fringe benefits constitute a labour cost for the employer.
- *Not directly linked with efforts:* Fringe benefits are not direct reward for the efforts made or the production given by an employee.
- *Beneficial to all employees:* Fringe benefits are a labour cost but its benefits should be made available to the entire labour force and not to a small group of employees.

Objectives of Fringe Benefits

- *To supplement direct remuneration:* Fringe benefits supplement regular pay of employed. It raises the total earnings of an employee and provides better life and welfare to him.

- *Employers prefer fringe benefits:* employers prefer this indirect remuneration to direct pay increase.
- *To retain competent employees:* Fringe benefits create satisfied labour force. In addition, the management can attract and retain competent personnel in the organisation by offering liberal packet of fringe benefits.
- *To develop good corporate/mage:* Fringe benefits help to develop a good corporate image.
- *To raise employee morale:* Liberal package of Fringe raises the morale of employees.

Limitations of Fringe Benefits

There are some limitations of Fringe Benefits. These are:

- Fringe Benefits may lead to unhealthy competition among employees
- The expected benefit may not be available if the monetary benefits are not adequately attractive to employees.
- The motivation may not be as per expectation if the implementation of the benefits scheme is not transparent.

Advantages of Fringe Benefits

There are certain advantages of Fringe benefits. These are:

- Fringe benefits provide support to remuneration paid to employees.
- Fringe benefits improve efficiency and productivity of employees.
- Fringe benefits act as an added attraction to the employees.
- Fringe benefits reduce monotony and fatigue of employees. They make employees efficient and co-operative for whatever organisational changes required to be introduced.
- Fringe benefits raise morale of the employees. They develop affinity for the organisation.
- Fringe benefits develop good corporate image and raise market standing of the organisation.

- Fringe benefits act as a motivating force. They motivate employees and induce them to work for the progress and prosperity of the organisation.

Types of Fringes/ Fringe Benefits

1. Payment for time not worked by the employee:
    - Holidays.
    - Vacations.
    - Leave with pay and allowances.
2. Contingent and deferred benefits:
    - Pension payment.
    - Group life insurance benefit.
    - Group health insurance.
    - Sick leave, maternity leave, child care leave, etc.
    - Suggestion/service award
    - Severance pay.
3. Legally required payments:
    - Old age, disability and health insurance
    - Unemployment compensation
    - Worker's compensation.
4. Misc. benefits:
    - Travel allowances.
    - Company car and membership of clubs, etc.
    - Moving expenses.
    - Child care facilities.
    - Tool expenses and meal allowances, etc.

SECTION-D
(Case Studies)

CHAPTER

8 Aska Cooperative Sugar Industries Ltd. (ACSIL)

Introduction

In the country map, Aska is known as Sugar Town and situated in the bank of river Rushukulya. In the nineteenth century (1854) the 1st sugar industry of South Asia was established at Aska of Ganjam district of Odisha by the Pyari Company of the then Madras city because of the fertility of soil. Since then the Aska is considered as Sugar Town. At the beginning its daily sugarcane crushing capacity was 100 tons. Fredric James Vian Minchin who was a retired soldier of German Army appointed as Manager of the Sugar Factory. He was popularly called "Minchin Saheb". Due to communication problem Pyari Company sold the factory to the Minchin Saheb in the year 1872. After the death of Minchin Saheb and his wife Sona Minchin in the 1903 and 1916 respectively the same factory was looked fter by some local people. But due to administrative and technological problem the same was closed down in the 1946. Then in the year 1956 a Society has been registered under the Odisha cooperative Society Act 1952 and the registered number is 1091 dated 17th August 1956. It started functioning from 31st August, 1956. The society obtained industrial license on 1st January, 1957 to set up a cooperative sugar industry and started preliminary activities followed by construction works. The factory has set up at Aska and the factory was inaugurated by the then Chief Minister of Odisha, Mr. Biren Mitra on the first day of commercial production i.e. 12th December, 1963. This factory was the first cooperative industry and first sugar industry in Odisha.

Objectives

(*i*) To encourage self-help, thrift and cooperation amongst members.

(*ii*) To acquire lands by purchase, lease or otherwise for cultivation of sugarcane and other crops and for the erection of buildings, machinery and for irrigation channels etc.

(*iii*) To inculcate amongst members improved modern methods of agriculture and cultivation of sugarcane and to supply seed materials, implements etc., for growing sugarcane and other crops and to promote agricultural and industrial education among members.

(*iv*) To manufacture sugar, jaggary and by-products out of the sugarcane supplied by the members and others and to sell the sugar to manufacture to the latest advantage.

(*v*) To establish a sugar manufacturing factory and manage it for that purpose.

(*vi*) To give advances to members on the security of sugarcane or sugar made out of their sugarcane and loans for raising their crops and the development of agriculture.

(*vii*) To install machinery for the utilization of by products and buy raw materials and sell finished products in the course of utilizing and marketing the byproducts.

(*viii*) To sell or otherwise dispose of the whole or any part of its business, assets or undertaking, including its factory buildings, machinery and lands for the benefit of the society or in the course of the winding up of the society.

(*ix*) To undertake such other activities as are incidental and conducive to the development of sugarcane growing and sugar manufacture.

In order to fulfil the above objects there are several subsidiary functions i.e. providing seeds, measures, fertilizers, pesticides etc. on loan basis and to arrange transportation of sugarcane from field to factory. It is the statutory obligation of the society to look after the welfare of the employees by providing medical facilities, education, accommodation and food at subsidiaries prices. A hospital, school and canteen are being run by the society.

The capacity of the industry is increased to 2500 MT per day from 27/02/1996 onwards. The industry has crushed 142786.782 MT of sugarcane during the year of audit against 146366.840 last year.

For utilizing one of its byproducts i.e. molasses, this factory has set up a distillery plant in Oct. 1974 with production capacity of 10000 BL (Bulk Liter) per day.

Bye Laws

The original bye-laws of the society have been produced before audit. The certificate of registration, aims and objects funds, shares, loans and advances etc. mentioned in the bye-laws was verified.

Management

According to clause No 26 of bye-laws of the society, the management shall vest in a Board of Directors consisting of-

(*a*) Three persons who shall be nominated by the State Government including Registrar of Cooperative Societies, Odisha.

(*b*) Six persons who shall be elected from the individuals (Producer Member) at the rate of one from each constituency. The constituencies shall be delimited by the management, subject to the approval of the Registrar of Cooperative Societies, Odisha.

(*c*) One shall be elected from the ordinary members.

(*d*) The Managing Director

(*e*) Any other person, if considered necessary by the committee subject to the approval of the Registrar in the interest of the society.

The elected Board of Management of the Society was suspended by the Registrar of Cooperative Society, Odisha vide order no. 6194, dated 22/03/1991. Since then the Management is vested with Registrar of Cooperative Societies, Odisha or the person nominated by the Government by invocation of law with effect from 22/03/1991. As the organization is a cooperative organization based on democratic principle, immediate steps need be taken to constitute the Board through election.

Board of Management

Vide letter no 11858/Gen dated 14/05/2004 of General Administration Department, Government of Odisha, the Collector-Cum-District Magistrate of Ganjam, Chatrapur has been appointed as Management in charge of the Aska Cooperative Sugar Industries Limited. Aska and the Board have been dissolved. The management in charge is continuing since then.

Proceeding of the Management

During the period of audit 21 meetings of the Board of Management of Aska Cooperative Sugar Industries Limited were held. The details of the agenda and resolution are verified with the proceedings of the meetings maintained in a separate register by the General Administration Department of the Organization.

Resources

The sugar industry has material and human resources according to its necessity to operate its plants without having any hindrance. It has about 150 acres of land for the complex and 15 acres for the township. Plant is getting its utilities i.e. power and water from Power Transmission Corporation of Odisha and the Odisha Health Department respectively to run its plants without any interruption. The raw materials required for the plant is sugarcane cultivated by the members of the society and bought out canes from out station. Fuel oil, wood and bagasse (by product of cane) are used for the running of steam generation plant.

Manufacturing Process

Sugarcane is transported from the cultivators by the factory and reached to the factory site by different means i.e. bullock cart, trucks, tractors etc. they are consequently conveyed to mechanically conveyor system to power machine called choppers the revolving knives of wheel help the canes into small pieces.

The chips are charged into cursor to extract the juice from the chips. The juice thereafter passed through screens and centre cleaners for separation of particles direct and other undesirables. After adding required chemicals i.e. lime, sulphur etc., and multiple evaporation process the juices are prepared to syrup of 60% solids. Then SO_2 gas are added with the solid syrup and processed for crystallization in vacuum pans. After passing three stages of massecuite finished products are ready for commercialize. The byproduct molasses are used for preparation of Alcohol. The industry is running for four to five months only in each year, i.e mostly from December to April and the rest of the year factory has remain shut down for maintenance purpose.

Staffing Pattern

The staffing pattern of the industry as approved by the Registrar of Cooperative Societies, Odisha, consists of eight Heads of Departments. Each department takes care of their respective section.

Sl. No.	Department	Heads of Department
1.	General Administration	Secretary
	(*i*) General Administration	
	(*ii*) Motor Vehicle	
	(*iii*) Watch & Ward	
2.	Accounts	Accounts Officer
	(*i*) General Accounts	
	(*ii*) Cane Accounts	
	(*iii*) Store Accounts	
3.	Personnel Management & Labour Welfare	Personnel Manager
4.	Cane Development	Cane Manager
	(*i*) Cane Development	
	(*ii*) Cane Extension	

5.	Marketing	Marketing Manager
	(*i*) Sugar & Miscellaneous Marketing	
	(*ii*) Cane Extension	
6.	Material Management	Purchase Superintendent
	(*i*) Purchase	
	(*ii*) Store	
7.	Engineering	Chief Engineer
	(*i*) Civil Engineer	
	(*ii*) Mill & Cane Carrier	
	(*iii*) Boiling House	
	(*iv*) Power House	
	(*v*) Boiler	
8.	Manufacturing	Chief Chemist
	(*i*) Office & Laboratory	
	(*ii*) Clarification	
	(*iii*) Pan Station & Crystallizer	
	(*iv*) Centrigugal & Sugar Bagging	
	(*v*) Distillery	

Under each department two categories of staff i.e. Permanent, Seasonal and Temporary have been appointed as communicated in memo no 2071 (8), dated 16/11/1984 of the Managing Director of the industry to all Heads of Department. The Heads of Department are provided with the following staff as per order cited above.

Sl. No.	Designation	Post Confirmed		
		P	S	T
1	General Administration	33	0	33
2	Account Section	15	0	15
3	Cane Accounts	0	0	0
4	Labour Welfare & T.O.	9	2	11
S	General Store & Purchase	12	2	14
6	Cane Development	82	69	151

7	Sugar Go Down	2	3	5
8	Watch & Ward	54	3	57
9	Engineering (C.E. OFF)	12	0	12
10	Mill House	26	24	50
11	Boiler House	25	35	60
12	Boiling House (Engg)	38	16	54
13	Power House	40	0	40
14	Workshop	22	0	22
15	Distillery, Warehouse, ETP	4	0	4
16	Civil	24	0	24
17	Manufacturing (SMP Office)	9	15	24
18	Boiling House (MFC)	0	31	31
19	PAN Station & Crystallizer	4	21	25
20	Centrifugal Machine	I	31	32
21	Dryer House	0	10	10
22	Marketing Section	6	0	6
23	Distillery	19	7	26
24	E. T. Plant	4	7	11
25	Bishram Bhawan	7	0.	7
26	D. M. Plant	1	I	2
27	Medical Sanitation	5	0	5
28	Printing Press	5	0	5
	Total	459	277	736

Source: Records of Aska Sugar Factory
P = Permanent S = Seasonal T = Total

Managing Committee

The company is managed by a Board of Directors. The details are 3 persons nominated by the Government of Odisha, inclusive of the Registrar Cooperative Societies, 6 persons who shall be elected from the individuals (producer members at the rate of one from each constituency - constituencies shall be determined by the management), the Managing Director deputed from the Government from Civil Service of All India Cadre of Odisha

Cadre, and any other person, if considered necessary by the board subject to the approval of Government in the interest of the society.

Flow Diagram of Aska Co-operative Sugar Industries Limited

Sugar
Juice
Imbibition
Basagesse (30%) by product to boiler as
Mixed juice
Filtered
Pre-
Milk of
Clarification
SO_2
Final heating to 100-
Clarifier for
Clarified
Sediment
Multiple effect
Vacuum
Syrup 60%
SO_2
Filter
Filter cake
Crystallization
A-
Curing in
Commercial

Apart from the above there are different committees have formed for the betterment and for administrative convenience such as—

Cane Development Committee

Managing Director
Chief Engineer (Mechanical)
Chief Chemist
Accounts Officer
Labour Welfare Officer
District Agriculture Officer
Cane Development Officer and
Representative of Cane Growers

Sales Committee

Managing Director

Secretary

Chief Chemist

Marketing Manager

Accounts Officer

Labour Welfare Officer

Representative of Recognised Employees Union

Committee for Fixation of Sugarcane Price

Registrar of Cooperative Societies, Odisha

Director of Agriculture and Food Products, Odisha

Joint Registrar of Cooperative Societies (Marketing) Odisha

Sugarcane Development Officer, Odisha

Managing Director

Representative of Cane Grower

Purchase Committee

Managing Director

Secretary

Chief Chemist

Chief Engineer

Materials Manager

Accounts Officer

Production Manager

Two Members from Recognised Employees Union

Staff Selection Committee

Managing Director

Secretary

Labour Officer

Concerned Head of the Department

The staffing pattern of the industry as approved by the Registrar Cooperative Societies of Odisha, there are 8 Heads of the Departments. They are the responsible of any commissions or omissions of their respective department. All are reporting to the managing Director.

Category-wise Man Power Statement

Sl. No.	Category	Total	Technical	Non-technical
1	Executive	75	55	20
2	Non-executive	514	195	319
	Total	589	250	339

Sources: From statistical data of Aska Cooperative Sugar Industry Limited

Out of total 75 executives 3 persons under deputation from the State Government, 514 non-executives inclusive of 319 seasonal (Skilled, Semi-Skilled and Unskilled) employees rcgualrised during the month of January, 2009. 9 persons are working as NMR workmen. 150 unskilled contractor workers are working. This number varies 10 per cent either side according to the need. In the sugar industry the responsibilities of employees are being defined to facilitate optimum work load and multi-skilling. This will result in better job satisfaction and no time for idle thinking. In this regard the organization has taken the assistance of external consultancy. Standard of performance has been developed for all jobs by arranging skill developed for all jobs by arranging skill development training programmes through external consultancy for different category of employees as per the requirement of factory from time to time. For utilizing the creative thoughts of the employees the organization has implemented suggestion scheme. Through suggestion schemes the department is encouraging the employees to use their creativity ideas for betterment of the organization and it helps the workers for their future growth and sense of involvement. Co-brotherly attitude among the employees are prevailing.

Trade Union

The present trade union (Recognised) of Aska Cooperative Sugar Industry Limited named as Aska Cooperative Sugar Industry

Limited (ACSIL) Employees Union was formed in 1963 with 135 members. Now it has 415 members and its own office bearers. Union is affiliated to All India trade Union congress (AITUC), The election for the office bearers and executive committee members of the union held once in two years. After expire of the tenure of the office bearers election will be conducted through secret ballot in a democratic manner. The objects of ACSIL Employees union are to organize the employees employed in ACSIL and promote their will being by all peaceful legitimate and constitutional methods. To create amongst the employees a healthy spirit of fellowship and cooperation and develop in them a proper sense of their duties, responsibilities and obligations. To promote cordial and harmonious relationship between the employees and their employer and secure redress for their difficulties. To secure fulfilment of the obligation of the employees to their employer for faithfully, efficient and punctual discharge of their duties and the maintenance of proper conduct discipline and respect for authority. To organize and render relief to employees during sickness, unemployment, old age, accident and death and also during the period of legitimate strikes or disputes with the employer and in accordance with the by law framed by the union from time to time. To provide legal assistance to employees in respect of all matters arising out of or incidental to their employment. To promote among the employees habits of thrift, temperance and cooperation and organize social insurance and cooperative societies. To provide opportunities for the educational and cultural development of employees and their leisure by organizing schools, reading rooms libraries, recreation, sports, entertainment etc. to organize medical relief, maternity and child welfare and promote the ideals of health and better living. Generally to cooperate with the endeavours of the Government local bodies, employers and public institutions to promote the welfare of employees. Apart from the above recognized union there are another unions named as ACSI Shramik Sangh bearing registration No 170JYP in the year 1996 affiliated to CITU. This union is having 99 members.

Membership

The employees working in ACSIL attained the age of 18 are eligible to the. member of Union. The employees till the grade of Supervisor/Junior Officer are eligible for its membership. The employees of different section will nominate two Executive members-from each section around 16 executive members including five Office Bearers of the Executive Committee of the Union. The Executive Committee consisting of the President, th Vice President, the General Secretaiy, the Assistant General Secretary and the Treasurer. In accordance with the provisions of the Indian Trade Union Act, 1926, the General Body of the union may admit not more than two honorary members, who are not actually employed or engaged in the ACSIL. The executive committee may device suitable machinery in all branches of ACSIL for enlisting membership and to carry on union activities in such places. Towards the membership the union generally deducted ₹ 60 from each member of the union through their salary slip once in a year. The annual accounts of the union shall be audited in accordance with the regulation 15 of Odisha Trade Union Regulation 1951 and shall be presented by the executive committee for adoption at the annual meeting of the general body. Any members who default in payment of his membership fee for a consecutive period of six months shall automatically forfeit his membership, all rights and privileges. But he can be readmitted on written request. If any members of the executive committee absent himself for sex consecutive meetings he shall be removed from the membership. Any officers' removal shall be on a motion of removal or a motion of no-confidence by members of the union formally moved at the meeting of the General Body of the Union. No motion of removal or no-confidence shall be declared to have been passed unless a majority of two third of the members present and vote in favour of it and the number of members present at the meeting of the General Body is not less than 50% of the total membership of the union.

Relationship of Trade Union with the Management

There is a harmonious relationship between the management and the trade union. The policy is being carried out by both the groups to maintain organizational culture and to achieve the organizational target. The union always emphasized the major growth of the company creating peace in the industry with safety environmental work field. Since a couple of years there is no agitation like *Gharao, Dharana*, Bearing black badge, slowdown of work by the employees/Union. No political functions have been taken care even at the level of announcement of the Central Trade Union. The policy of management is to satisfy the needs of the workers through dialogue and the union will not take any risk of agitation to settle their immediate needs. The union nominate its members for satisfy committee, school committee, welfare committee, cultural functions, grievances committee and other social activities. The work committee is formed through election by all the unionized employees of different departments and the equal number of representatives will also be nominated by the management among officers to form a complete Work committee. The office bearers of the union are closely associated and guided the committee members for the smooth functioning.

Social Responsibility of the Union

To improve the Socio culture of the localities, the union plays a major role to strengthen the economic and social condition of the nearby villagers. The cultural functions are very often carried out under the guidance of the leaders to encourage the villagers as well as to improve the social culture of the union members.

Unions View On Management

The management of ACSIL always believes up on transfer of views with the union leaders. The problems related to the workmen are being mutually settled down in a cordial atmosphere. It is observed that there is no such agitations created by the union people since 2005 the major problems are settled down by means of tripartite agreement. The policy of the management is somewhat flexible. The labour policy of the management evenly accumulated and constantly uninformed. All the category of employees are equally treated.

CHAPTER

9 Indian Rare Earth Ltd. (IREL)

Introduction

Indian Rare Earth Ltd. (IREL) was incorporated on August 18, 1950 as a private limited company jointly owned by government of India and the government of Travancore subsequently in year 1963; it became a fully-fledged government of India undertaking under the administrative control of department of atomic energy.

IREL is a pioneer in the field of mining and processing of beach sand minerals such as Ilimenite, Rutile, Zircon, Monazite, Garnet and Sillimenite etc. it is operating three mining and mineral processing units viz. at Chavara (Kerala), Manavalakurchi (Tamil Nadu) and Chatrapur (Odisha). It is also operating a chemical plant, rare earth division at Udyogamandai (Kerala) for processing monazite and producing rare earths compounds with several diversification plans in progress, including modernization of existing plant and machinery, the company is poised for further growth from its current level of sales turnover of approx. ₹ 2,900 million with foreign exchange earning of approx, ₹ 1,000 million. Apart from meeting the domestic demand IREL caters to the international markets viz, USA, Canada, Austria, UK, France, Norway, Germany, Japan, South Korea, China, Ukrain etc., even under several global competitions.

Besides providing raw materials to the basic industries and the core sector of the country, IREL is also plays a strategic and unique role in the strategic atomic energy program of the country. It is the only producer of the monazite mineral, containing thorium and uranium. Uranium is being extracted at the R.E. division of IREL and is used in the nuclear reactors as fuel, while thorium is considered as the fuel for the future nuclear energy programme of the country. The Zircon mineral being produced by IREL is the raw material for the ufacture of zircaloy tubes used for filling uranium fuel in the nuclear reactors.

Since incorporation of the company at Mumbai in 1950 the company has grown steadily during the post 50 years and the sales turnover of the company on 2000-2001 reached all-time highly of race 2591 million. The company has been a significant earner of valuable foreign exchange for the nation. IREL has been exporting its product to advance countries like USA, Canada, Austria, UK, France, Norway, Germany, Japan etc. in the decade export earnings have raised from ₹ 229 million to an impressive ₹ 1000 million.

IREL has built up a corporation image in the world market as a reliable supplier of beach minerals and rare earth compound. The ISO 9002 certification received by all four operation units of IREL bears further testimony to commitment of the company for equality and customer satisfaction.

The company's pride lies in its harmonious cordial relationship with employees for several years. The production plants of IREL have adapted highest level of safety standards along with environmental friendly technique to exploit the obediently available minerals from the beaches of eastern and western part of Indian peninsula.

The management of the company is interested with a group of highly and experienced directors down from different field's technical marketing finance R & D and mining aspects of its operations.

Established as rare earth company beach sand minerals business has continued to be the main stay of IREL and is expected to remain so in the current changing environment of liberalization which has promoted global participation and entry private entrepreneurs into the field of beach sands minerals.

IREL management is adapting dynamic and innovative policy to maintain its lead in world market.

LOCATION

Chavra

The plant is located in Kollam district of Kerala State. The state is located at a distance of about 15 km from Kollam which is the district headquarters.

Manavalakurchi

The Manavalakurchi plant is located in the Arabian Sea coast of Kanyakumari district of Tamil Nadu State. The state located at distance of about 18 km from Nagercoit the district headquarters.

Oscom

The minerals belt running over a coastal length of nearly 18 kms with a total area of over 26 sq. km between Gopalpur in the south and Rushikulya river in the north is estimated to contain about 230 million tons of raw sand with 20-25% heavy minerals and is expected to last for about 100 years. To exploit these natural resources, IREL has built and integrated industrial complex known as OSCOM (Odisha Sands Complex) near Matikhalo village about 8 km south of Chatrapur town (Odisha) in the year 1984.

Location (IRE)

I.R.E. Ltd., OSCOM is situated near Matikhalo village 10 km away from Chatrapur, the headquarters of Ganjam District and 30 km away from Berhampur one of the major cities of Odisha. It is also situated near Gopalpur sear port. The Bay of Bengal is nearly one kilometer away from this factory. The river Rushikulya which flows a distance of 10 km away from the factory is going to meet all the future water requirements of the factory.

Category-wise Manpower

To deal with the performance appraisal of IRE Ltd, Matikhal, Chatrapur in district Ganjam of Odisha the category-wise man power statement is highly required. This has been explained in Table 9.1.

Table 9.1 Category-wise Man Power Statement

Sl.No.	Category	Technical	Non-technical	Total
1	Officers	131	48	179
2	Management Trainees	—	02	02
3	Dy Officers, Dy Engineers	42	25	67
4	Official Staff	—	22	22
5	Skilled Workman	408	—	408
6	Unskilled	—	288	288
7	Security Guards	—	46	46
8	Helper	—	24	24
	Grand Total	581	455	1036

Source: From the records of IRE Ltd.

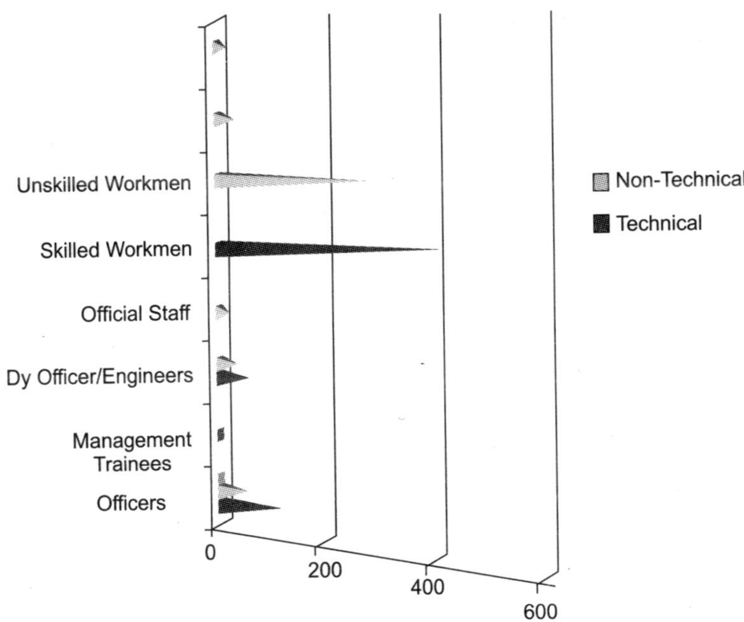

Diagram of Man Power Statement

Before Performance Appraisal

Before Performance Appraisal of the staff the behavior attitude of the staff, regarding salary, work style, environment etc. are to taken into due consideration, according to the information collected at the time of primary information. The views of the total staff regarding their pay are illustrated in the Table 9.2:

Table 6.2 Views of the Staff Regarding their Pay.

Particular	Strongly agree	Slightly agree	Slightly disagree	Strongly disagree	Total
The most important thing about my job is the pay	13%	30%	35%	22%	100%
Organization regarding my contribution	12%	52%	24%	12%	100%
The staff who gets best pay work to get more for them.	09%	19%	26%	46%	100%
Hard work is not necessary rewarded	37%	44%	12%	07%	100%

Source: Compiled from the questionnaire

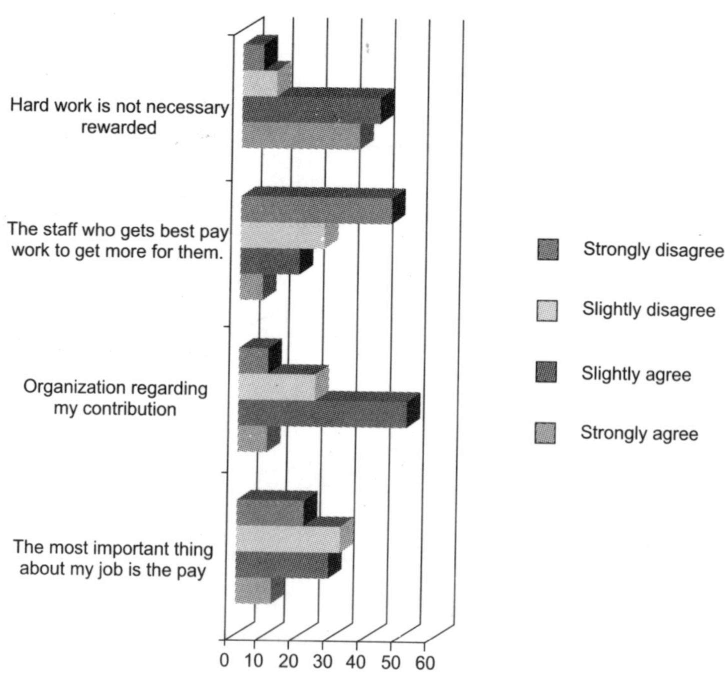

Opinion About Work Performance

To study the performance standard of the employees of IRE Ltd, a Government undertaking the work performance of the staff, along with the right man for the right job, work satisfaction is illustrated in Table 9.3.

Table 9.3 Opinion of the Employees Regarding their Work

Sl. No.	Statement	Strongly agree		Slightly	Strongly	Percentage
1	I know about my work objectives in detail.	41%	43%	11%	05%	100%
2	My work is difficult to perform	07%	17%	35%	41%	100%
3	Supervisor help me at the time of need	45%	37%	11%	07%	100%
4	The equipment supplied are best to perform the work	38%	33%	19%	10%	100%
5	I have performed the work at highest level	52%	37%	05%	06%	100%
6	The job are clearly understate	62%	26%	09%	03%	100%

Source: Compiled from the questionnaire

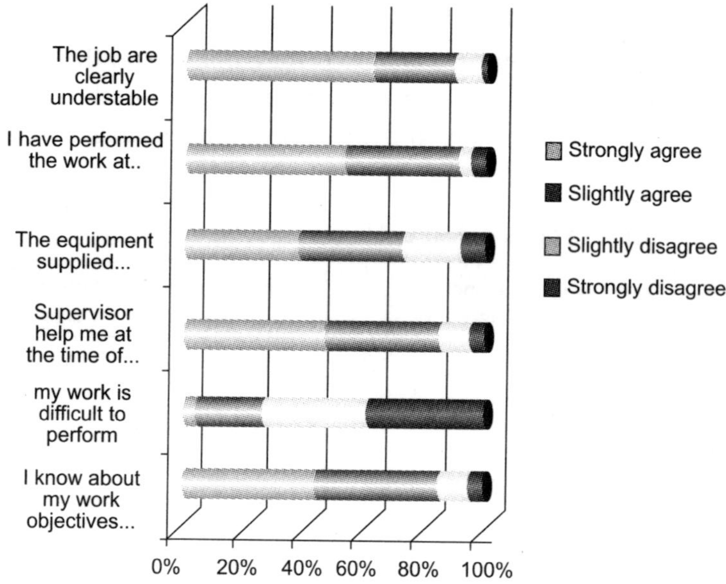

Understanding of Meaning of Performance Appraisal by the Employees (IRE Ltd.)

The staff should know about the meaning, objectives, system and detail about the performance appraisal and how it is helpful for the measurement of work standard regarding payment of wages/salary and for the promotion of the staff. They must have very clear idea about the work performance as per time and job specified for the purpose. Further they know about degree of performance i.e. 360 degree of performance. How many staff/ employees are well aware of the work performance are explained in the Table 9.4.

Table 9.4 Understanding of Work Performance by the Staff

Sl. No.	Particular	Percentage		Total Percentage
		Positive	Negative	
1.	Regular meeting with boss	82%	18%	100%
2.	Performance appraisal on review	77%	23%	100%

...(Contd.)

3.	Setting objectives	71%	29%	100%
4.	Training Need	67%	33%	100%
5.	Personal Development plan	66%	34%	100%
6.	Performance rating (regarding pay)	57%	43%	100%
7.	FeedBack Policy	73%	27%	100%

Source: Compiled from the questionnaire

As per Table 9.4 most of the staff i.e. 82% staff meets the boss in the office time to overcome the difficulties. But only 57% are not in favour of performance rating regarding payment of pay.

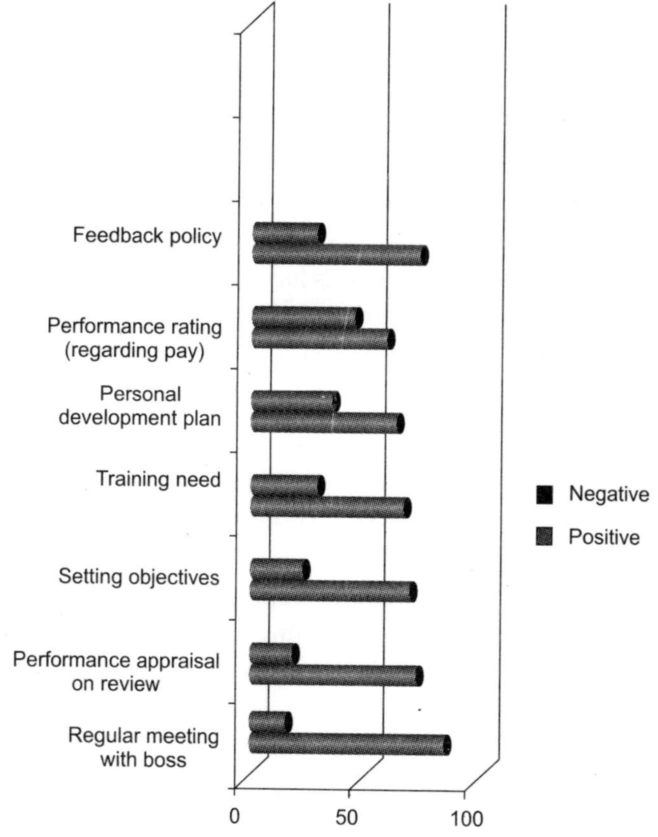

Various Departments of Oscom (Odisha Sands Complex)

Production Department	Mining, Mineral Separation Plant, Thorium Plant.
Service Department	Utility Central Workshop, Central Store, Auto Cell, Fire Station, Security, Medical, Physics Unit, Ware House.
Administration Department	Human Resources, Internal Audit, Purchase Market.
Technical & Research Department	Safety and Training, Technical Service, Project Cell.

Oscom Governed under Various Act & Rules

- Mines Act, 1952
- Mines and Mineral Development Act, 1957
- Mines concessional Rule
- Mines conservation & Development Rule
- Automatic Energy Factories Rules, 1996

Rare Earth Division (Udyigamandal)

The Rare Earth division is located at Udyogamandal near Kochi (Cochin) Kerala state. The plant is located on the bank of river Periyar at Udyogamandal in floor Panchayat.

Mission

To harness beach sands in an environmentally and socially responsible manner for efficiently producing minerals and their traditional and innovative value added products of world class quality, that are used to make increasing Ely superior/novel products required by customers.

To play a dominant role in developing domestic rare earths market by producing and/or marketing the quality value added products to realize maximum potential of rare earth in range of apples.

To build a professional, creative and committed workforce and nature an environment, that fosters learning, sharing and development.

Control Process

Process control: Collection of feeds in various stages of processing and after analysis forwarding, a report there on for being better quality production as well as control whole process. This work is done by shift wise in respect of DWSP, SMP, MSP AND TP.

Quality control: Independent collection analysis are reporting of find MSP product sample at ware house for quality control analysis and reporting of find Thorium plant product samples for quality control analysis of chemical received are central stores as per purchase order.

Research and development: Mineral processing: various mineral processing studies are carried out times to times with available labs, more equipment for improvements of quality and quantity of products, feasibilities studies, optimisation of process parameters developmental studies, equipment such as available for conducting the above studies.

Technical Services Diagram

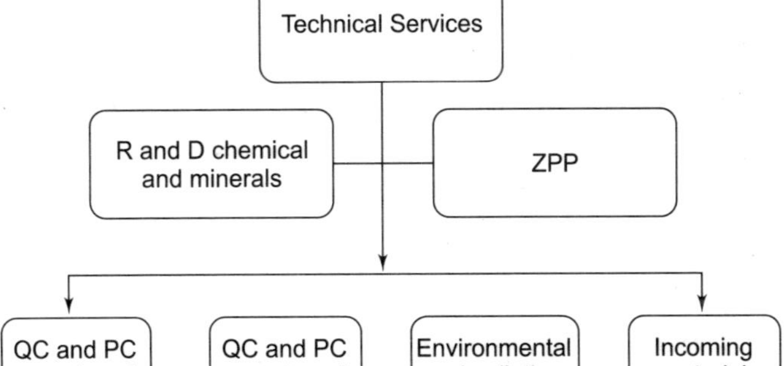

PC : Process Control
QC : Quality Control
R&D : Research and Development
TP : Thorium Plants
ZPP : Zirconia Pilot Plants
MSP : Mineral Separation Plant

ZPP (Zirconia Pilot Plant)

In this plant one of the find product of MSP named zircon, is further process to a value added product known as high pure Zirconium oxide and stabilized Zircon Oxide.

Capacity of same plant is 3.5 T/annum process Zircon.

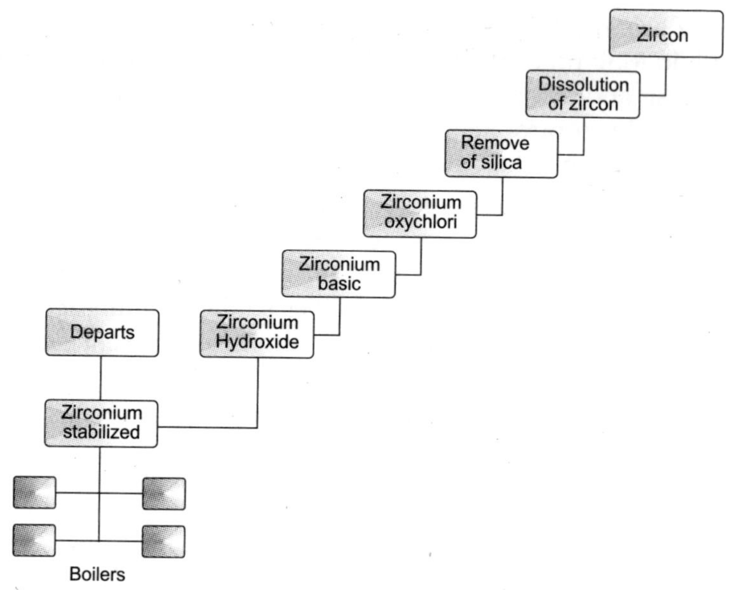

Process of Zirconia Plant Operation

- Boiler-1 Running Hours
- Coal Consumption
- Stream Produced in MT
- Oil received Water Level

Style of Management

Primary, the organization of OSCOM believes in the democratic style or management. However, in many occasions, the organizations also adopt the participative style of management.

Trade Union

At present, Rare Earth Employees union is the one and only trade union operating in the organization of OSCOM. It is affiliated to INTUC. It is a recognized union. The union was established on 1st May 1980. This union has been registered on 11th September 1980 under the name and style of Rare Earth Employees having registration number of 1298/80. 90% of the employees are member of the union. Arun Kumar Nahak as the Persident of the existing union is concerned. The activities of the union are concerned. The activities of the union are confirmed within the organization only.

Environment Policy

(Odisha Sand Complex) OSCOM has its own pollution control. The organization also has its own environment development policy. With regard to environment development, OSCOM has received different awards trophy in the form of shield from different bodies. OSCOM has also received the inter unit best environmental/greenery award from the CMD (Chairman cum Managing Director).

CHAPTER

10 Jayashree Chemicals Ltd. (JCL)

Introduction

Jayashree Chemicals Limited (JCL) was established in the year 1962 by M/S Bangur Brothers of Calcutta. It has started its production on 4th August 1967. Jayashree Chemicals Limited (JCL) is situated at Ganjam town in the district of Ganjam, Odisha on the bank of river Rushikulya and is about 10 km from Chatrapur, the district headquarters of Ganjam. The river Rushikulya is a southern side and bay of Bengal on the eastern side of the factory. It is well connected by rail line of South Eastern Railway and by road on National Highway No. 5. The company produces caustic soda, hydrochloric acid, calcium, hydro chloride and other industrial chemicals. These are supplied to Rayan mills, paper mills, soap and textile industries, petrochemical manufacturers, water works, steel plants, oil refineries, etc. as raw materials for these industries, The raw-materials required for the company are sodium chloride, graphite, chemical, and mercury. The chemical required are soda ash, barium carbonate or chloride and others which are used in brine purification process and prepared indigenously. Mercury is imported from neighbouring countries.

The manufacturing process is largely manual as such jobs require low-leveled skill. However, the manufacturing process is a complex electro chemical process. This process involves making of saturated salt solution, its purification removal of unwanted impurities and electrolysis with heavy direct current, again purification and concentration of caustic soda washing, drying, compressing and refrigerating chlorine to produce liquid chlorine synthesis of hydrochloric Acid using hydrogen and chlorine and manufacture of calcium hydrochloride using lime survey. The machineries used in the manufacturing process are age-old depreciated and worm out consequently the quality of products is very poor and unable to meet the challenge of competitor's products.

The structural pattern of Jayashree Chemicals Limited (JCL) is noteworthy, since the whole system can be classified into three categories:

(*a*) Administrative

(*b*) Technical

(*c*) Commercial

These three branches, function under the Deputy Chief Executive. The chief executive being located at the head office Calcutta. He is the top most and the sole policy making authority of the Organization. The deputy chief executive is directly connected with the plant and responsible for optimum utilization of human and other resources and achievement of organizational goal. He is assisted by heads of different department of JCL. The works executive is the head of the technical branch looks after the administration and production target of the whole organization and answerable to the Deputy Chief Executive only.

The personal function of the organization is supervised and controlled by the manager (administration) a top level executive. He is answerable to deputy chief executive. The Manager (HRD), Deputy Manager (HRD) and medical officer directly answerable to manager (Administration). The works accountant, a top executive enjoy the same status as that of manager (administration) as the organization structure is a horizontal one. The manager (administration) is responsible for the day-to-day administration of the company including transport, security etc. The three chief engineers are the heads of their respective units and are concerned with the output of their respective units. They are assisted by their Deputy Chief Engineers. All the three Chief Engineers (Chemical, Mechanical

& Electrical) are directly answerable to the Deputy Chief Executive.

The personnel department of the company looks after personnel industrial relations and labour welfare aspects is headed by the Manager (Administration) assisted by Manager (HRD) Dy Manager (HRD) Management trainees and other sub-ordinate officials.

It has been observed that the span of control in the technical department is wider than other departments and in it the chain of command is also very lengthy since any decision of top management has to cross five hierarchical levels to reach junior management level. The structural pattern in purely based on line and staff pattern. The technical department which is directly with production is considered as line and rest of the department are considered as staff as they indirectly help production process.

Human Resources Management Practices in JCL

Manpower procurement otherwise known as staffing is a multi-step process. It consists of determination of manpower needs, recruitment, selection, placement and orientation. In JCL all these functions are meticulously carried by the HRD department.

Manpower Forecasting

The first step of procurement is manpower need or forecasting which means future manpower requirement.

At present the company is not giving proper attention to manpower forecasting programme. It is because the company is an old one and is without sufficient forecasting data. Besides this the labour turnover in the factory is not satisfactory. Still the company has divided its whole working personnel into three categories.

(*a*) At present the company is not giving proper attention to manpower forecasting programme. It is because the company is an old one and is without sufficient forecasting data. Besides this the labour turnover in the factory is not satisfactory.

(*b*) Still the company has divided its whole working personnel into three categories size like:

(*i*) Executive

(*ii*) Staff

(*iii*) Workers.

The company has specified their minimum qualification which is beneficial for planning and analyzing job description of human resource.

(*c*) The executive category is further sub-divided into Senior Executive, Middle Executive and Junior Executive. Similarly the staff category is divided into Supervisory, Clerical and worker category. Worker category is divided into highly skilled, skilled, semi-skilled and un-skilled. The same is explained in the Diagram below.

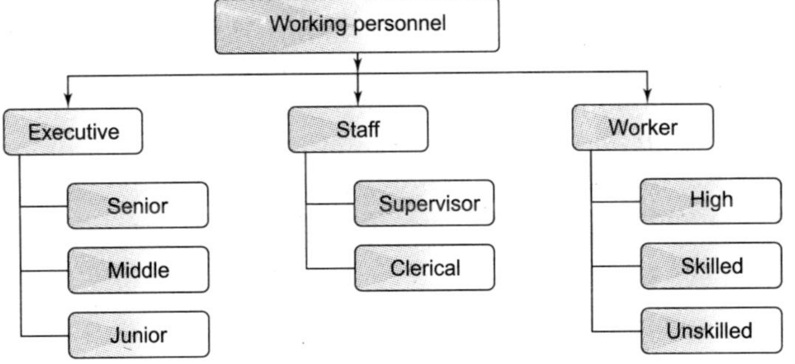

Recruitment Policy

The company at present does not have any specific written recruitment policy and their framework of recruitment programme is influenced by various external forces. The pressure groups which influence the policy are:

(*i*) Government

(*ii*) Trade Union

(*iii*) Political Power

(*iv*) Sons of Soits

The company strictly follows the employment exchanges (Compulsory Notification of Vacancies) Act, 1969 for workers on staff and supervisory categories. For unskilled and semi-skilled jobs the trade union influences its pressure by making agreements with management. So, the management gives employment opportunity to the unskilled and semi-skilled workers as per the agreement with the trade union.

Source of Recruitment

The company normally depends on:

(*i*) Employment or Labour Exchange

(*ii*) Advertisement

(*iii*) Casual Labour Force Chart.

For the source of recruitment. Besides these the company also relies upon internal source by giving promotions and transferring the personnel from one unit to the other. It gives employment opportunities to the dependents of the deceased employees on rehabilitation scheme. The company depends on the Employment Exchange as a source of recruitment for Supervisory, skilled and semiskilled and staff cadre position. For middle order and junior level management cadre the company advertises for filling in the vacancies in national, state and local newspapers to select suitable candidates from open market.

Manpower Development

The company gives high regard for human capital. It believes in human development sice its establishment. It gives scope to junior employees to rise up by improving their work efficiency and develop themselves within the organizational like procedure.

At present the company is not conducting any systematic induction programme for newly appointed employees. As a matter of fact fresh intake of manpower is stopped. The company says that it has a surplus staff in non-technical branches and had adopted Voluntary Retirement Scheme (VRS) thereby downsizing the manpower to a great extent. Even in technical branch there is a stagnation of staff The downsizing and stagnation manpower at different levels led to frustration and dissatisfaction among different workers.

Perquisites and Fringe Benefits

The JCL at present is extending certain employee benefits and services like housing, transport, health, recreational facilities, education, social security etc. as per the norms prescribed in different laws in force in the country.

Wage Scheme

Regarding the wage structure of the company it is prepared in the lines recommended by Wage Board for Heavy Chemicals and Fertilizer Industries. The company also makes negotiations with the union at an interval of every three year for necessary modifications and alterations in wage structure. It also considers the prevailing wage rates in different local industries similar in nature while preparing its wages. The structure of the company has been divided into ten grades for different categories of employees of Grade I to Grade X. apart from basic wage, the company pays Dearness Allowance (D.A), Additional Dearness Allowance (A.D.A), Variable Dearness Allowance (V.D.A) and other allowances like washing allowance, coconut oil allowance, medical allowance, special allowance etc., to its employees. The company pays wages to its employees on the seventh day of every month as per the provisions of payment of wage Act 1936 at different countries of the plant at different periods.

References

Armstrong Michael & Baron Angela, "Performance Management—A Strategic and integrated approach to achieve success," Jaico Publishing House, Mumbai, 2007.

Armstrong, M. (1995), "A Handbook of Personnel Management Practice", Kogan page Ltd. London.

Bache, J.F. (1995), Performance Appraisals—Let's avit appraising & begin reviewing steeping up performance ed. Benson, G., Jaico Publishing House, Mumbai.

Baird, L., Beatty, RW. & Schneier, C.E (1983), "The Performance Appraisal Source Book", Human Resource Development Press, Massachusetts.

Cascio, W.I. (1995), Managing Human Resources', Mc-Graw-Hill, New York.

Daniels, A.C. (1990), "Bringing Out the Best in People", Mc-Graw-Hill. Inc. New York.

Ferris, GR & Gilmore D.C. (1995), *Appraisals Everyone can agree on stepping up performance*, ed. Benson, G., Jaico Publishing House, Mumbai.

Ginow, M. A. (1990), "Appraising the Performance of Professionals". *Employees, Designing Performance Appraisal Systems*, ed. Mohrman, A.M., West S.M.R. & Lawlar, EE, Jossy-Bass Publishers San Francisco, CA.

Gumming, M.W. (1972), "The Theory and Practice of Personnel Management", Willam Heineman Ltd., London.

Heneman, H.G. (1989), "Personnel/Human Resource Management", Universal Book Store New Delhi.

Heyel, C. (1973), "The Encyclopedia of Management", Reinhold Publishing Corporation Newyork.

Hill, J. (1997), "Managing Performance", Grower Management Work Books, Famborough England.

Jain, S.C. and Mathur, N.D. (1988), "Readings in Performance Appraisal", RBSA Publishers, Jaipur.

Levinson, H. (1976), "Appraisal of What Performance?", *Havard Business Review* July.

Maier, R.N. (1976), "The Appraisal Interview: Three Basic Approaches", University Associates Inc, California.

Mc Gregor, D.(1957), "An Uneasy Look at Performance Appraisal", *Havard Busines Review*, May-June.

Megginson, L.C. (1967), "Personnel; A Behavioral Approach to Administaration", Richard D. Irwin Inc, Chicago.

Misra Rakesh Kumar, Ph.D. Thesis—"Performance Appraisal of Employees working in difficult Industrial Sector".

Mufeed, S. (1998), *Indian Journal for Training and Development*, Vol. XXVIII, No. II, April-June.

Pareek, U. and Rao, T.V. (1993), "Designing And Managing Human Resource System", Oxford and IBH Publishing Co. Pvt. Ltd., New Delhi.

Pattabbraman, S. (2001), "Not Just for allocation" A&M, Spectrum Publication, New Delhi, Vol-XIII, NO. III.

Randell, G.A. (1974), "Staff Appraisal", Institute of Personnel Management, London.

Ratnam Venkata C.S., "Industrial Relation"—Oxford University Press. YMCA Library Building, New Delhi-110001, 2006.

Rauch, E. & Frisch, M.H. (1985), " Win Win Performance Management Appraisal" John Wiley & Sons, New York.

Schuler, RS. & Huber, V.L. (1990), "Personnel and Human Resource Management", West Publiching Company New York.

Schuler, RS. (1987), Personnel & HRM", West Publishing Company, New York.

Subbarao, P. (2000) "Personnel and Human Resource Management", Himalaya Publishing House, Mumbai.

Venkatesh, D.N. and Jyothi, P, "Human Resource Management"—Oxford University Press—YMCA Library Building, New Delhi-110001, 2006.

Werther, W.B. & Davis, K. (1993), "Human Resource and Personnel Management", McGraw -Hill international edition New York.

Index